Put English To Work

LEVEL 3

INTERACTION AND COMPETENCIES FOR JOB SUCCESS

W9-BMX-944

CAROLE ETCHELLS CROSS

SERIES ADVISOR
CAROLE ETCHELLS CROSS

CONTEMPORARY BOOKS

a division of NTC/CONTEMPORARY PUBLISHING GROUP
Lincolnwood, Illinois USA

Publisher: Steve VanThournout
Editorial Director: Cindy Krejcsi
Executive Editor: Mary Jane Maples
Editor: Michael O'Neill
Contributing Writers: Laura Franklin, Jeffrey P. Bright
Director, World Languages Publishing: Keith Fry
Art Director: Ophelia M. Chambliss
Cover and Interior Design: Michael Kelly
Fine Art Illustrations: Adam Young
Line Art Illustrations: David Will
Production Manager: Margo Goia

ISBN: 0-8092-3357-6

Published by Contemporary Books,
a division of NTC/Contemporary Publishing Group, Inc.,
4255 West Touhy Avenue,
Lincolnwood (Chicago), Illinois 60646-1975 U.S.A.

90 DH 0 9 8 7 6 5 4 3

Contents

About This Book v

Unit 1 Reading Help Wanted Ads 1
Reading help wanted ads • Talking about work experience and objectives • Scanning ads for specific information • Understanding the parts of a business letter • Acquiring and evaluating information
• Functions: Talking about past experience; stating short-term plans • *Not . . . anymore* • Future with
going to • Past tense of regular and irregular verbs

Unit 2 Job Search Strategies 15
Identifying sources of information about job opportunities • Reading simple job descriptions
• Identifying occupations and corresponding skills and education • Reading an organization chart
• Understanding systems • Functions: Expressing disappointment; expressing cause; talking about
habitual past activities • Exclamations • Clauses with *because* • *Used to*

Unit 3 Work History and Résumés 27
Discussing one's employment history • Using a time line • Understanding the organization and
components of a basic résumé • Organizing information • Functions: Giving and getting permission;
expressing preference; making offers • *Do you mind if . . . ?* • Verbs with infinitives • *Would you like . . . ?*

Unit 4 Interviews and Applying for Jobs 39
Arranging for interviews and applying for jobs • Identifying qualities of a successful job applicant
• Understanding appropriate questions and responses in an interview • Teaching others/helping
others learn • Functions: Expressing inferences; talking about tentative plans; talking about experience
• *Must* • *Might* • Present perfect with *ever*

Unit 5 Paychecks and Deductions 51
Understanding paychecks and deductions • Understanding and completing a W-4 form • Figuring
personal allowances from a worksheet • Acquiring and evaluating information • Computation skills
• Functions: Comparing quantities; explaining • Comparatives • Superlatives • *More . . . than,
less . . . than, bigger /smaller . . . than*

Unit 6 Company Rules and Instructions 63
Understanding company rules and policies • Reading memos • Understanding announcements and
notices • Interpreting and communicating • Teaching others/helping others learn • Functions: Expressing
obligations; expressing preferences • Present perfect with *never* • *Would rather*

Unit 7 Teamwork 75

Understanding the basic principles of effective group interaction • Identifying leadership skills
• Reading and creating an action plan • Participating as a member of a team • Negotiating • Leadership
• Functions: Reporting what someone has said; clarification and confirmation • Reported speech
• Present perfect with *for* and *since*

Unit 8 Conflicts at Work 87

Identifying effective ways to resolve work conflicts • Identifying sources of conflict and ways to avoid it
• Understanding policies on employee behavior and harassment • Negotiation • Working with cultural
diversity • Participating as a member of a team • Functions: Apologizing; suggesting; explaining
• *I'm sorry* • *Ought to* • Present perfect and simple past contrasted

Unit 9 Meetings and Reporting Progress 99

Reporting progress on activities • Understanding interaction in meetings • Reading schedules, charts,
and graphs • Allocating time • Allocating material and facility resources • Allocating money
• Allocating human resources • Functions: Expressing ability and inability; reporting how much is completed;
suggesting; expressing certainty • *As much/many as* • Present perfect and simple past
• *I'm sure (that) . . .* • Present conditional

Unit 10 Safety Procedures 109

Understanding safety signs and instructions • Identifying appropriate protective clothing for specific tasks
• Identifying safe work procedures • Interpreting and communicating • Teaching others/helping others learn
• Functions: Warnings; talking about ongoing activities; talking about future consequences of present acts
• Gerunds • Present perfect continuous • Future conditional

Picture Dictionary 121

Appendix 122

About This Book

Put English to Work is a seven-level interactive workplace-literacy course for students of English as a second or foreign language. The series spans the entire range of levels usually taught in ESL/EFL programs—from the beginning-literacy level to the high-advanced level. A communicative, competency-based program, *Put English to Work* features an integrated syllabus focusing on workplace competencies, general English-language skills, communicative functions, form, and culture. The content of each text has been carefully planned to meet the curricular, instructional, and level requirements of California's state standards for adult ESL programs.

The format of *Put English to Work* is designed for maximum flexibility and ease of use. Teachers in a variety of programs—from vocational ESL and workplace ESL programs to general ESL programs with a school-to-work focus—will find this series ideal for their instructional needs. In addition, teachers who work with multilevel classes will find these texts useful with almost any combination of levels because of the cross-level coverage of a number of the most important workplace topics. *Put English to Work* consists of the following components:

- Seven student books, from Literacy Level to Level 6
- Seven teacher's guides, one for each level
- Seven audiocassettes, one for each level

Each student book contains a Picture Dictionary at the back—an additional resource offering teachers a variety of strategies for vocabulary building. The teacher's guides contain extension activities, sample lesson plans, and suggestions on adaptation of the materials to a number of different teaching styles and programs, from integration of grammar to using the materials in multilevel settings. The teacher's guides also contain the tapescripts for the audiocassettes, which are available separately.

The philosophy behind *Put English to Work*—spelled out in greater detail in the teacher's guides—is interactive and competency-based. The series places a strong emphasis on developing the four language skills—listening, speaking, reading, and writing—in conjunction with critical thinking, problem solving, and computation skills. An important feature is the incorporation of the SCANS competencies, developed by the Secretary's Commission on Achieving Necessary Skills in a project sponsored by the Department of Labor. In addition, the series focuses on a great number of the competencies within the Comprehensive Adult Student Assessment System (CASAS).

Skills are taught within an integrated framework that emphasizes meaningful and purposeful use of language in realistic contexts to develop communicative competence. Target language, structures, and functions are presented in contexts that are relevant to students' lives. Students need to learn strategies and skills to function in real-life situations—in particular, those related to job search and the workplace. Other situations and life-skill areas are covered as well, notably health, family, and community resources.

The cultural focus of *Put English to Work* not only presents aspects of U.S. culture that many students need to come to grips with, but also allows for a free exchange of ideas about values and situations that people from different cultures naturally view differently. In the process, students learn about the culture that informs the U.S. workplace while understanding that their own cultural perspectives are intrinsically valuable.

Level 3 of *Put English to Work* is geared toward learners at the low-intermediate level. Students at this level can function satisfactorily in English in survival situations; they can participate in basic conversations, and they can already comprehend conversations with unfamiliar vocabulary. A certain number of the skills of Level 2 are reviewed in Level 3, and teachers with classes of mixed intermediate-level students may wish to use Level 3 in conjunction with the Level 4 text. With mixed beginning-level and intermediate-level classes, teachers may also wish to use the Level 2 text with this level. Suggestions for use of these levels are provided in the teacher's guides for these levels.

Level 3 focuses on the development of intermediate language skills, document literacy, critical thinking, and problem solving through the presentation of realistic workplace contexts, along with frequent use of collaborative-learning activities. These activities involve working in teams with a team leader, a team recorder, and a team reporter. When students have specific assigned responsibilities, they are able to perform group work more cohesively and effectively. This translates into more effective cooperative learning. Collaborative team activities provide a means for emphasizing teamwork and interaction skills, which are a major focus of Level 3. In addition, students begin to do some paragraph writing at this level, though punctuation is not taught explicitly. Paragraph-writing activities involve a preparation stage with guided writing of individual sentences. In Level 3, most vocabulary is taught through glosses, preparing students to read definitions in a dictionary.

The SCANS competencies targeted in Level 3 are the following:

Allocating material and facility resources
Allocating time
Allocating money
Acquiring and evaluating information
Interpreting and communicating information
Organizing and maintaining information
Leadership
Negotiating
Teaching others
Participating as a member of a team
Working with cultural diversity
Understanding systems

Acknowledgments

The authors and publisher of *Put English to Work* would like to thank the consultants, reviewers, and fieldtesters who helped to make this series possible, including Gretchen Bitterlin, San Diego Community College, San Diego, CA; Ann de Cruz, Elgin Community College, Elgin, IL; Greta Grossman, New York Association for New Americans, New York, NY; Bet Messmer, Educational Options, Santa Clara, CA; Michael Roddy, Salinas Adult School, Salinas, CA; Federico Salas, North Harris Montgomery County Community College, Houston, TX; Terry Shearer, Houston Community College, Houston, TX. Special thanks to Mark Boone.

Unit 1
READING HELP WANTED ADS

Openers

Look at the pictures. Match the jobs to the ads. Find these things:

blowtorch   computer   keyboard
visor   company logo

Kham is reading the help wanted ads in the newspaper. Do you ever look through the want ads for a job? What do you need to understand when you read ads in the newspaper?

1 Listen and Think

Listen. Then answer the questions with a partner.

1. What kind of job does Kham want?

2. Why does the manager ask him to call back?

3. Does Kham have enough information about the job in the ad?

4. What additional information does Kham need?

2 Talk to a Partner

Step 1. Someone is calling about a job. Practice the conversation with a partner.

> A: Hello. I saw your ad in the paper **for an employee for your video store.**
>
> B: Oh yes. Could you tell me something about your work experience?
>
> A: Well, **I worked in a camera store for five years. I sold cameras and accessories.**
>
> B: When did you leave that job?
>
> A: **Two years ago.** After I left **the camera store,** I worked **in a department store downtown. I sold men's clothing.**
>
> B: Are you available to work **in the evening**?
>
> A: **Sure. No problem.**

Step 2. Now choose an ad from the ones below or on page 3. Have a conversation like the one above. Use your own information.

3 Read and Think

Step 1. Read the text below.

Al Johnson, Kham's job counselor, told Kham to look for specific types of information in want ads.

Here is some of the information in want ads:
1. The type of job **2.** The salary or pay **3.** The work week and working hours **4.** What work experience or education you need **5.** Any personal tools or equipment you need **6.** The location or phone number of the workplace

Step 2. With a partner, look at the ads below. Which ads have the information given above? Circle the information and write the number next to it.

Warehouse - Inventory control. FT, night shift, 4:30–12:30. Call 356-0968.

Computer programmer for suburban company (in Anaheim). $30,000. Call 762-7495.

Clerk-typist. Experience with computers required. Must know word-processing software. Call 487-9073.

Vocabulary

inventory control counting and recording company products

FT (abbreviation) full-time; thirty-five to forty hours a week

night shift working hours that start after 4:00 or 5:00

word-processing software a type of computer program for letters and documents

Step 3. Ads are usually under general categories. Read the ads below. Circle the general categories and underline the jobs.

Restaurant - Wait staff, FT and PT, Cooks, exp'd only. Call 780-6532.

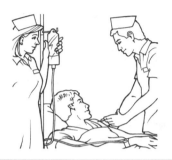

Health Care - Registered nurses needed for Lane Hospital. Call 874-0987 or write to P.O. Box 7685.

Construction - Construction Manager. Immediate opening. 5–10 years exp. required. Call (316) 984-0987.

Clerical - Typist needed for large corporation in suburbs. Must type 60 words per minute. Call (708) 956-9654.

Engineer - Tunnel engineer. Structural engineer with 15 years of experience in tunnel design. Write to . . .

Hablo español (note tilde over "n")

Education - Spanish teacher with state K8 certificate for elementary school in suburbs. Call (619) 985-8345.

Vocabulary

wait staff waiters and waitresses, servers in a restaurant

PT (abbreviation) part-time; under 30–35 hours a week

exp'd. (abbreviation) experienced, to have experience

exp. (abbreviation) experience

registered nurse nurse with certification

clerical related to office work (typing, filing, answering telephones)

Step 4. Ads are usually under general categories. Read the ads below. Circle the general categories and connect them with a line to the jobs.

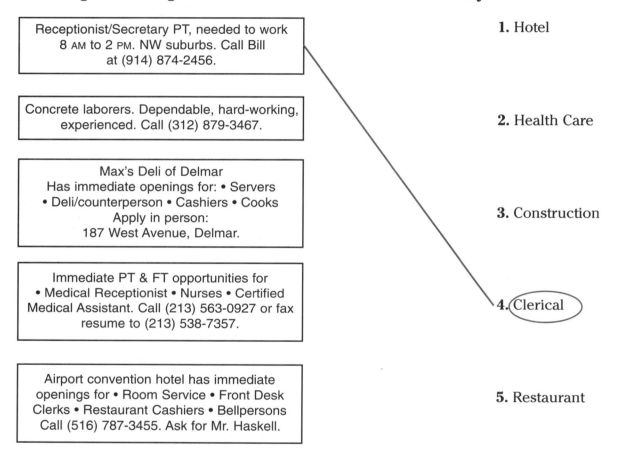

Receptionist/Secretary PT, needed to work 8 AM to 2 PM. NW suburbs. Call Bill at (914) 874-2456.

Concrete laborers. Dependable, hard-working, experienced. Call (312) 879-3467.

Max's Deli of Delmar
Has immediate openings for: • Servers
• Deli/counterperson • Cashiers • Cooks
Apply in person:
187 West Avenue, Delmar.

Immediate PT & FT opportunities for
• Medical Receptionist • Nurses • Certified Medical Assistant. Call (213) 563-0927 or fax resume to (213) 538-7357.

Airport convention hotel has immediate openings for • Room Service • Front Desk Clerks • Restaurant Cashiers • Bellpersons Call (516) 787-3455. Ask for Mr. Haskell.

1. Hotel

2. Health Care

3. Construction

4. Clerical

5. Restaurant

Vocabulary

bellpersons people who work in a hotel and help guests with their suitcases and luggage

concrete laborers a person who works with concrete (a building material)

deli/counterperson a person who works in a deli (a small business that sells prepared foods and sandwiches); a counterperson serves customers in a restaurant or deli

dependable (adj.) reliable, said of someone you can depend on

servers waiters or waitresses (wait staff)

Practice

Complete the sentences with the words below.

clerical   wait staff   night shift   inventory control   construction

1. Henry got tired of his job on the _____*night shift*_____ , so he found a day job.

2. At the warehouse, Joanna does the _____, and she has to know exactly how much of everything the company has.

3. Jobs as a typist, a secretary, an office clerk, and a receptionist are examples of _____ jobs.

4. The Logan Restaurant is looking for _____ and is seeking people who are friendly and comfortable with customers.

5. Terrelson Company is hiring _____ workers to work on the new office building downtown.

4 Put It in Writing

Step 1.   Think of a job you know. Imagine you want to hire someone for that job. Write three sentences: (1) the kind of person you need, (2) the hours, and (3) the pay.

Example: *I need a cook. The hours are from 9 in the morning to 6 in the evening. The pay is $15,000 a year.*

1. _____

2. _____

3. _____

Step 2.   Now write the qualifications for the same job.

Example: *The successful candidate must know U.S. and Latin American cooking. This person must have 3 years experience as a cook.*

_____

_____

_____

Step 3.   Put your sentences together and write an ad on a separate sheet of paper. Use any abbreviations you know. Then, with a partner, compare your work.

5 Listen and Speak

Step 1. Listen. Kham found an interesting job possibility. But there's a problem.

Kham: There's a good job as a warehouse manager in Torrance.

Al: Really? That's great! You worked as a warehouse
manager before you came to the U.S., right?

Kham: Right. But Torrance is too far for me. I don't have a car.
I live in L.A., and I don't have the time to take the bus.

Step 2. Practice the conversation with a partner.

Step 3. Create an ending to the conversation.

Student A: Suggest a way to solve Kham's problem.

Student B: Do you agree with your partner? Take a position for or against. Change roles.

Here are some ideas. Think of more ideas of your own.

Kham could move to Torrance.   Kham could buy a car.

Step 4. With another pair of classmates, compare your ideas. Do you agree or disagree?

6 Read and Write

**Step 1. Read Kham's cover letter. Kham wrote it to answer an ad. The labels show the parts
of the letter.**

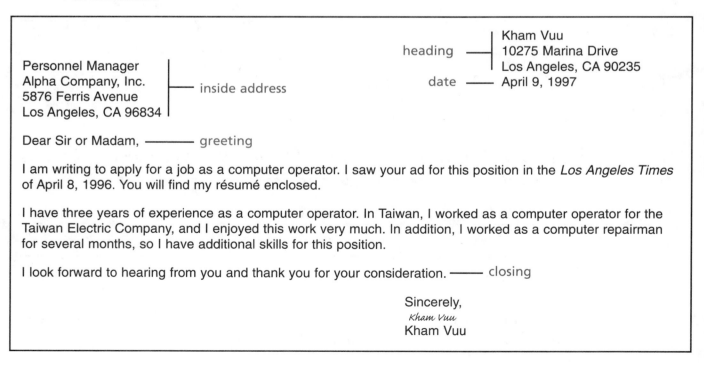

heading ——— Kham Vuu
10275 Marina Drive
Los Angeles, CA 90235

date ——— April 9, 1997

Personnel Manager
Alpha Company, Inc. ——— inside address
5876 Ferris Avenue
Los Angeles, CA 96834

Dear Sir or Madam, ——— greeting

I am writing to apply for a job as a computer operator. I saw your ad for this position in the *Los Angeles Times* of April 8, 1996. You will find my résumé enclosed.

I have three years of experience as a computer operator. In Taiwan, I worked as a computer operator for the Taiwan Electric Company, and I enjoyed this work very much. In addition, I worked as a computer repairman for several months, so I have additional skills for this position.

I look forward to hearing from you and thank you for your consideration. ——— closing

Sincerely,
Kham Vuu
Kham Vuu

Step 2. Choose an ad from pages 3–4. Complete the sentences below or write sentences of your own. Use the current date and the name of your local newspaper.

1. I am writing to apply for a job as a(n) _____.

2. I saw your ad for this position in _____ of _____. You will find my résumé enclosed.

Step 3. Complete the sentences below or write sentences of your own.

1. I have _____ years of experience as a(n) _____. In _____, I worked as a _____ for _____, and I enjoy this work very much.

2. In addition, I worked as a(n) _____, so I have other skills for this position.

OR:

1. I have no experience, but I have a number of important skills: I can _____, _____, and _____.

2. Also, I am a quick learner, and I am sure that I will learn to work as a(n) _____ very quickly.

Step 4. Copy your sentences onto a separate sheet of paper. Put them into two paragraphs. Then add a heading, the date, and a closing. Use Kham's letter as a model. With a partner, compare your work.

Form and Function

1 I don't work at the factory anymore. I left that job two weeks ago.

| not . . . anymore | I, you, we, they | don't work there **anymore.** |
| | he, she, it | doesn't work there **anymore.** |

Examples

Roberta **doesn't smoke anymore**. She quit last year. Jorge **doesn't live in Colombia anymore**. He came to the U.S. two years ago.

Practice 1

A. Listen. Circle True or False.

1. Jack still works downtown.   T   (F)

2. Janet doesn't smoke anymore.   T   F

3. Ron isn't unemployed anymore.   T   F

4. Jane's still a nurse.   T   F

5. Anne doesn't live in New York anymore.   T   F

B. Think of three things you don't do anymore. Write three sentences on a separate sheet of paper. Then tell a partner.

Example: *I don't work as a waitress anymore.*

2 I'm going to call about the job when I get home.

I'll call	**when** I, you, we, they **get** there. / **when** he, she, it **gets** there.
(I'm going	**before**
to call)	**after**

Examples

When Rick gets home, he'll read the newspaper.
After he reads the newspaper, he'll watch TV for a while.
He'll look through the help wanted ads **before he throws the paper away.**
He always looks through the help wanted ads **before he throws the paper away.**

Practice 2

A. Listen. Circle True or False for each sentence. For each false sentence, change the incorrect words.

                        after
1. Juan's going to call ~~before~~ he drives his children to school.   T   (F)

2. Alice's going to call when she gets home from her evening classes. T   F

3. Pierre's going to call before he leaves for the same class.   T   F

4. Paula's going to call after her daughter leaves for school.   T   F

Who is going to call first? _____

Who is going to call second? _____

B. Look at Jorge's schedule for tomorrow. What is Jorge going to do? When? Write four sentences.

7:00 get up	9:00 get to work, talk to boss
8:00 take car in to garage	about vacation dates
8:30 go to work	1:00 have lunch with Rosa
	6:30 meet Julio, go bowling

1. *Jorge's going to get up at 7:00.* _____

2. _____

3. _____

4. _____

5. _____

C. Write out your schedule for tomorrow. Then tell a partner what you are going to do.

3 A: I worked in a camera store five years ago. I sold cameras.
   B: When did you leave that job?

work > work**ed**			
I you he, she, it	work**ed**	Where did	I you he, she, it we they	work?
we you they	work**ed**		I, you, he, she, it we, they	didn't work

sell > **sold**			
I you he, she, it	**sold**	What **did**	I you he, she, it we they	sell?
we you they	**sold**		I, you, he, she, it we, they	didn't sell

Examples

I **worked** in Detroit last year. I **was** a mechanic. I **fixed** cars and motorcycles.
My friend Jim **bought** a new car last year. I **gave** the car a tune-up.
A: **Did** you **check** the oil in his car? B: **Yes**, I **did**. But I **didn't check** the tires. I **checked** everything
  else.

Practice 3

A. Listen. Circle the correct answer.

1. reads   (read)

2. starts   started

3. call   called

4. work   worked

5. answer   answered

6. puts   put

B. Fill in the blanks with the correct forms of the verbs in parentheses. Use any other words in parentheses correctly in combination with the verbs.

1. A: When (Jerry) (work) _____did Jerry work_____ for IBM? B: In 1979.

2. René (go) _____ to the store an hour ago to buy a newspaper.

3. Yesterday, Sam (have) _____ a talk with an employment counselor about a job.

4. I (not buy) _____ a car last year because I (not have) _____ enough money.

5. Enrique (sell) _____ jewelry in his old job in Guatemala.

6. A: Why (you) (leave) _____ your last job?

   B: I (leave) _____ to go back to school.

7. Kristina (drive) _____ to work every day for her last job because

   it (be) _____ in the suburbs.

C. Work with a partner. The chart below shows what several people did last week and when. Some of the information is missing. Ask questions and complete the chart. Use the correct forms of the verbs.

Student A: Look at this page.　　　**Student B:** Look at page 12.

Example:
B: What did **Jim** do last week?
A: **He bought a car.**
B: Oh. When did **he** do that?
A: On **Tuesday.**

Person	Action	Day
Jim	buy a car	Tuesday
Frank		
Kathy	break her leg	Monday
Anna		
Bill	have a party	Saturday
Jane		

Work with a partner. The chart below shows what several people did last week and when. Some of the information is missing. Ask questions and complete the chart. Use the correct forms of the verbs.

Student A: Look at page 11.   **Student B:** Look at this page.

Example:
A: What did Frank do last week?
B: **He left his job.**
A: Oh. When did **he** do that?
B: On **Thursday**.

Person	Action	Day
Jim		
Frank	leave his job	Thursday
Kathy		
Anna	work on her car	all week
Bill		
Jane	go to Boston	Monday

D. Role-play.

Student A: Choose one of the ads from this unit. Tell a partner you called about the ad. You scheduled an interview for next week. You need a job, but you are worried about your English.

Student B: Try to help your partner. Compliment his/her English. Tell your partner he/she shouldn't worry.

Example: A: I called about the job as an electrician yesterday. I scheduled an interview for next week. But now I'm worried my English isn't good enough.
B: Your English is fine. You shouldn't worry. Your interview will go OK.

Add your own ideas and change roles.

Putting It to Work

1 Pair Work

Step 1. With a partner, listen and fill in the missing information for these help wanted ads.

Distribution company wants someone with shipping and receiving experience. Pack orders, move stock, do _____ inventory control. _____ _____ Some computer experience. Call (213) 378-8974.

Company is seeking a clerk typist to type letters using _____ software, do filing, and answer phones. Must have _____ and computer experience. We offer _____ package. Send your resume to:

Busy suburban repair shop needs exp'd _____. Friendly atmosphere with benefits. Call for appointment:

Bartender, _____ Minimum experience required. Call for interview: _____.

Welding supervisor. _____ Bilingual preferred. Send resume to: Jo

Construction - Foremen, laborers. _____ _____ Call _____.

Hotel desk clerk, _____ Experienced preferred, will train. Apply in person only. Super Motel, Highway 8.

Step 2. Would you like one of these jobs? Which jobs can you do? Put numbers by the ads in order of your preference. Then talk to your partner. Which jobs would your partner like? Which jobs can he or she do? Ask.

2 Pair Work

Step 1. Role-play. Choose one of the jobs in the ads above.

Student A: Imagine you really would like the job, and there is a lot of information you want to find out.
Ask about • salary • the possibility of an interview • any other information you need

Student B: You are the employer. You already have a large number of candidates, and you don't want to talk to any more. You want to end the conversation quickly.

Example: A: Hello. I'm calling about the ad for a desk clerk.
B: All right. Give me your name and phone number and I'll call you back.
A: Oh. Could you just tell me the salary?
B: The salary is about _____. What's your name?
A: My name is _____. I could come in for an interview anytime.

Step 2. With the new information, rewrite the ad on a separate sheet of paper.

3 Group/Class Work

Step 1. In a group, choose any of the occupations you know. Work together to brainstorm qualifications, salary, and other information for a help wanted ad. Provide information for all these topics:

1. The type of job
2. The pay
3. The working hours

4. What work experience or education you need
5. Any personal tools or equipment you need
6. The location of the workplace

Step 2. Write the ad with your group, but leave some of the information out of the ad.

Step 3. One person from your group will write your ad on the board. Then role-play a telephone conversation about your ad with a student from a different group. You are the employer, and the other student is calling about the ad. The other student will ask you about the information that is not in the ad.

4 Culture Work

In your native country, how do you approach possible employers about a job? Look at the two situations below.

1. Paul Wengler saw a want ad and went to the company. He wanted to talk to someone about the job. He met a secretary and asked her about it.

Paul: Hi. My name's Paul Wengler. I saw your ad for a computer programmer. Could I possibly talk to the manager about it?
Secretary: He's not here right now. He won't be back till later this afternoon.

2. Sylvia Mitchell wrote a letter about a job. She included a résumé with her letter. Then she called a week later. She wanted to talk to someone about her letter and résumé.

Sylvia: Hello. My name's Sylvia Mitchell. I saw your ad for an administrative assistant, and I sent you a résumé. I wanted to ask if you received it.
Personnel Manager: Oh. Let me see. Oh yes. Sylvia Mitchell? Yes, I have it right here.

How would these situations end in your native country? How do you think they would end in the United States? Discuss this with the class.

Openers

Look at the picture. Point to these things:

wrench   toolbox   punch press
factory   sign

Jorge needs to find a job right away. He's talking to a friend because he doesn't know where to look. In Colombia, Jorge used to work in a factory.

1 Listen and Think

Listen and take notes. Then answer the questions with a partner.

1. What's Jorge's problem?

2. Why can't Jorge find a factory job?

3. What kinds of things can Jorge do?

4. Should Jorge move because he can't find a factory job?

2 Talk to a Partner

Step 1. Practice the conversation with a partner.

> A: I know **how to repair many kinds of equipment.** I can **use computers a little.** I know how **to type,** also.
> B: You could find a job as **a repairman** or **a computer operator.** Or maybe you could work as **a mechanic.** You could work as **a typist.**
> A: Oh, that's a good idea.
> B: The **garage on Franklin Avenue** is looking for **a mechanic.** Also, they need **computer operators** and **typists** at **a data processing company downtown.**

Step 2. With a partner, brainstorm a list of things you know how to do. Include things you did in your native country.

Step 3. Think of job possibilities for your partner. Tell your partner your ideas.

Step 4. If possible, think of specific places in your community for these jobs. Make a list of possibilities with your partner.

3 Read and Think

Step 1. Read the following job descriptions. What do people in these jobs work with? Circle the words that give you the answers. The first example is already circled.

Auto mechanic. An auto mechanic works on (cars.) Mechanics <u>repair and replace parts</u> and keep cars in good working order. For this job, a complete knowledge of cars, parts, and general automotive mechanics is very important. Mechanics sometimes replace simple parts, like spark plugs, and other times they have to overhaul the engine or replace the carburetor.

Secretary. A secretary is responsible for many things in an office. Secretaries type letters, keep files, go to meetings, answer telephones, and, in general, organize the office. Usually, secretaries must type very fast, often at 50, 60, or even 70 words per minute. Secretaries also know word-processing software (computer programs for letters and documents).

Computer operator. A computer operator uses many kinds of computer programs and knows computers very well. Often, computer operators must install computer programs on company computers. Sometimes, computer operators also have to know something about programming.

Vocabulary

automotive mechanics the study of cars, how they work, what parts are in them, etc., for mechanics, people who fix problems with cars

spark plugs parts of a car that make a spark; the spark lights gasoline

overhaul to fix, change completely

engine the engine makes the car run

carburetor the carburetor mixes gasoline and air and sends it to the engine

files papers and documents organized and kept in folders

install computer programs to put a program on a computer

Step 2. Read the job descriptions on page 16 again. Which words or phrases tell about job skills? Underline all of the words or phrases you find. The first phrase is already underlined.

Step 3. Are there any jobs, skills, or activities you know well in the descriptions on page 16? Put parentheses ( ) around the jobs, skills, or activities you know.

Step 4. Do your classmates know these jobs, activities, or skills? Try to find two classmates with a knowledge of any of these. Write their names below.

_____   _____

Practice

Complete the following sentences with the correct words.

1. An auto mechanic must have a good knowledge of ___*cars*___.

2. Sometimes, mechanics replace simple parts, like _____.

3. Mechanics often do complicated work; for example, they sometimes have to overhaul

_____.

4. When a mechanic has to replace the _____, it is an expensive job.

5. Secretaries often have to keep _____ for important papers and documents.

6. Computer operators work with computer programs. Sometimes, they have to

_____.

4 Put It in Writing

Step 1. **Write the answers to the questions below.**

Examples: Do you like to work with your hands? _Yes, I do._

What activities do you really like? _I like to make things with my hands._

I like to repair cars.

1. Do you like to work with your hands? _____

2. Do you like to read? _____

3. Do you like to work with people? _____

4. What activities do you really like? _____

5. What jobs or skills do you know? _____

Step 2. **List three jobs you know. Do you like these jobs?**

_____   _____   _____

Step 3. **In a group, compare your answers. What jobs do your classmates like? What activities do they like?**

5 Listen and Speak

Step 1. **Listen to Jorge's conversation with the manager of a small electronics company.**

Jorge: I'm looking for work, and I'm interested in your company. I have a lot of experience as a repairman.

Manager: I don't think we're hiring right now.

Jorge: What kinds of equipment do you use? Do you have punch presses? I used to repair punch presses in Colombia.

Manager: You did? Well, we do have punch presses, but I don't think we need any repairmen right now.

Step 2. **Practice the conversation with a partner.**

Step 3. How can Jorge learn more about the company? Create a positive ending to the conversation. Choose one of the ideas below or make up your own. Role-play the ending with your partner.

1. Jorge has his résumé with him, and he shows it to the manager. "Here's my résumé."

2. Jorge asks the manager the name of the personnel manager of the company. "Could you tell me . . .?"

3. Jorge gives the manager his business card and asks for the manager's card. "Here's my business card."

4. _____

5. _____

6 Read and Write

Step 1. Read the parts of the organization chart of Stansfield Data Company. One part is on this page. Another part is on page 20.

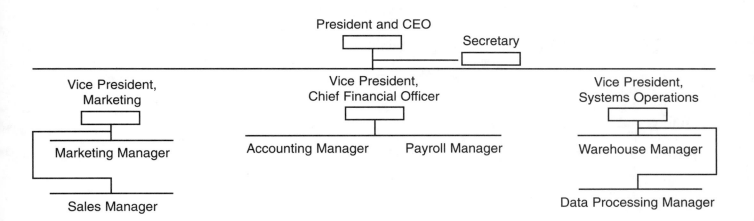

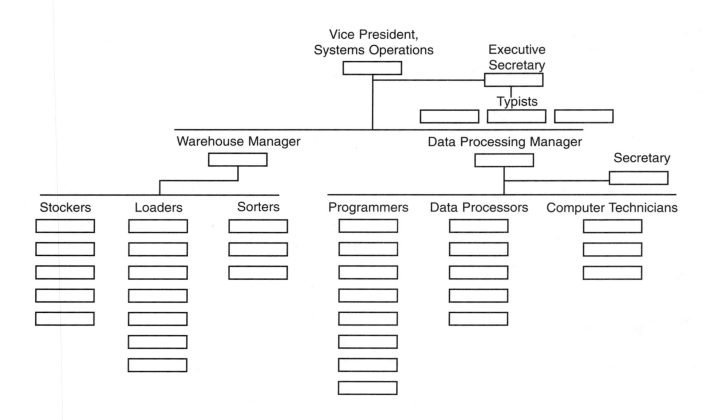

Step 2. Copy the jobs onto a separate sheet of paper. Put them under these categories:

Managerial   Clerical   Technical   Manual

Example:

Managerial	**Clerical**	**Technical**	**Manual**
President	Secretary	Data Processor	Stocker

Form and Function

1 The company hired someone else. What a disappointment!

What a	disappointment! shame!	**What**	great weather! lousy weather!
What a	great job! lousy job!	**What**	nice children! interesting books!
What an	interesting job!		

Examples

A: I didn't get the job. B: Oh, **what a shame!**

What great weather! It's beautiful outside! **What nice children!** They're all so good!

A: I have to read technical documents all day. B: **What a difficult job!**

Practice 1

A. Listen. Circle the word(s) you hear.

1. (What a)   What an   What   **3.** What a   What an   What

2. What a   What an   What   **4.** What a   What an   What

B. Choose the correct responses to the sentences below. Write the responses on the lines.

What a disappointment!	What a great job!	
What an interesting company!	What lousy weather!	What great weather!

1. I didn't get the job I wanted. *What a disappointment!* _____

2. This job pays $15.00 an hour, and the work is easy. _____

3. It's sunny and warm outside. _____

4. It's cold and rainy today. _____

5. This company makes educational films. _____

C. Role-play a short conversation about a job you would like. Tell a partner you applied for the job but didn't get it. How do you feel about that? Tell your partner.

Example: A: There's a really good job at the telephone company. I applied for it, but I didn't get it. What a disappointment! B: Oh, that's too bad! (OR) Oh, what a shame!

2 It's difficult to find work because no one is hiring right now.

> Pablo is looking for an office job **because he worked in an office in Mexico.**
>
> **Because he worked in an office in Mexico,** Pablo is looking for an office job.

Examples

Jorge looked for a factory job **because he worked in a factory in Colombia.**
Because Maria had evening classes, she had to find a job during the day.

Practice 2

A. Listen. Then complete the sentences.

1. Why did Jerry look for a factory job? ___*Because there was*___ an ad in the paper.

2. Why did Jerry call about an office job? _____ candidates for the factory job.

3. Why did Ron call about the same job? Because _____ skills.

4. Why did Jerry prefer the factory job? _____ about computers.

   Who will get the office job? _____ Why? _____

   _____

With a partner, compare your answers.

B. On a separate sheet of paper, write sentences matching the phrases below.

Example: Alice went home early because she needed to relax.
  (OR) Because she needed to relax, Alice went home early.

A	B
Alice went home early	because he hates his job as a waiter
Geraldo answered an ad for an electrician	because she is unemployed
Maria talked to an employment counselor	because he likes to work with machines
Harold took a computer course	because she is looking for a job
	because she needed to relax
	because he needed computer skills

C. Why are you studying English? On a separate sheet of paper, write about your reasons.

D. Talk to a partner. Where are you from? Why did you come to the United States? Explain your reasons.

Example: I'm from Angola. I came to the United States because there was a civil war there.

3 A: In Colombia, I used to maintain and repair drill presses.
B: And you worked on cars, too, right? You could be a mechanic.

I, you, he, she, it, we, they	**used to**	work as a mechanic.
I, you, he, she, it, we, they	**didn't use to**	drive to work.
Did I, you, he, she, it, we, they	**use to**	work as a mechanic?
What did I, you, he, she, it, we, they	**use to**	do?

Examples

I **used to** work as a mechanic, but now I work as a restaurant manager.
A: **What did** you **use to** do before? B: I **used to** work in a warehouse.
I **didn't use to** drive to work, but now I do.
A: **Did** you **use to** take the subway every day? B: Yes, I **did.**

Practice 3

A. Listen. Do you hear *used to* or *used?* Circle the words you hear.

1. used to   (used)
2. used to   used

3. used to   used
4. used to   used

5. used to   used
6. used to   used

B. Work with a partner. Ask questions and complete the chart. Student A: Look at this page. Student B: Look at page 24.

Example:

B: What did Fred use to do?
A: He used to work as a doctor.
   (OR) He used to be a doctor.
B: Where did he use to work?
A: In Chicago.

Person	Job	Place
Fred	Doctor	Chicago
Mary		
George	Electrician	Los Angeles
Jane		
Dan	Cook	Houston
Amy		

Work with a partner. Ask questions and complete the chart. Student B: Look at this page. Student A: Look at page 23.

Example:

A: What did Mary use to do?
B: She used to work as a teacher.
   (OR) She used to be a teacher.
A: Where did she use to work?
B: In New York.

Person	Job	Place
Fred		
Mary	Teacher	New York
George		
Jane	Typist	Santa Rosa
Dan		
Amy	Firefighter	Detroit

C. **What did you use to do before you came to the United States? Where did you use to live? Write three sentences.**

1. _____

2. _____

3. _____

D. **Fill out the chart below for four classmates. What did your classmates use to do in their native countries? Ask them. Then try to think of a job they could do in the United States.**

Example:

A: What did you use to do in Iran?
B: I used to sell jewelry.
A: Maybe you could work as a salesperson here.

Name	Job in Native Country	Job Possibilities in the U.S.

Putting It to Work

1 Pair Work

Step 1. Listen and take notes. With a partner, complete the list of skills for the jobs below.

Electrician

Knowledge of electrical equipment
Knowledge of electronic parts

Nurse

Basic knowledge of medicine
Taking blood pressure

Office worker

Knowledge of computers
Knowledge of word-processing software

Auto mechanic

Knowledge of cars and parts of cars
Knowledge of models of cars

Step 2. Ask your partner if he or she knows how to do the things above. Make a list of the things your partner can do.

Example:

A: Do you know how to use a computer?
B: Yes, I do. Do you know how to repair cars?
A: No, I don't.

Step 3. Compare your list with the list of another pair of classmates. Can you think of any job possibilities for your classmates? Try to think of at least one idea for each person.

2 Group/Class Work

Step 1. In a group, read the information about the following companies. Which companies fit your skills?

Company/Business: Technitrak, Inc.

Type of company: Producer of computers

Contact Person: Sandra Halliday

Job Title: Personnel Manager

Types of jobs: Electricians, engineers, assemblers, technicians, secretaries, salespeople

Company/Business: The Old Inn

Type of company: Restaurant

Contact Person: Ron Jackson

Job Title: Restaurant Manager

Types of jobs: Assistant manager, cooks, waiters, waitresses, hostesses, dishwashers

Company/Business: Wells Group

Type of company: Producer of medical supplies

Contact Person: Jaime Alvarez

Job Title: Human Resources Manager

Types of jobs: Assembly-line workers, foremen, secretaries, receptionists, salespeople

Company/Business: Spring Insurance

Type of company: Insurance company

Contact Person: Sarah Kowalski

Job Title: Personnel Director

Types of jobs: Salespeople, typists, telemarketers, administrative assistants, data processors

---

Step 2. With your group, talk about the skills necessary for different jobs in these companies. On a separate sheet of paper, list these skills.

Step 3. Tell the group about your own skills. List in order the skills needed at the companies above. Put your strongest skills first and your weakest skills last.

Step 4. Which companies would you like to work at? Which kinds of jobs would you like to have? Tell the class and give your reasons.

3 Culture Work

Discuss these questions with the class: In your native country, how do you find out about job possibilities? How is it different in the United States? Do you find jobs . . .

Through **word of mouth?**

Through **your family?**

Through **school** or **a university?**

Unit 3
WORK HISTORY AND RÉSUMÉS

Openers

Look at the pictures. Find the following things:

a welding helmet   an assembly line   a calculator   a mechanic

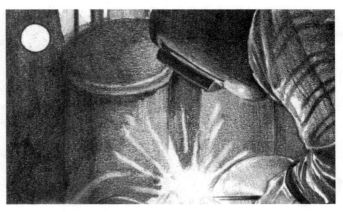

Kham is still looking for a job. Now, he's thinking about his résumé. What's the best way to present the facts about his work experience on paper?

1 Listen and Think

Listen and number the pictures above. Under the pictures, write the names of the jobs.

2 Talk to a Partner

Step 1. **With a partner, practice the conversation with the job counselor.**

A: What kind of job are you looking for?
B: Well, I'm hoping to get a high-paying job
   in industry. Do you mind if I show you my résumé?
A: Not at all. Oh, I see. You used to work for a printer?
B: Yes, that's right.
A: What did you do there? I don't see that here.
B: I did plate making.
A: You should add that to your résumé. How long did
   you do plate making?
B: About five years.
A: So then, you're looking for a job in printing?
B: No, I'd like to do something different.

Step 2. **Practice the conversation again. Use your own information.**

Step 3. **Ask your partner the dates of his/her jobs or work experience. Take notes. Check your partner's notes.**

Example: A: When did you work as a typist?   B: From 1993 to 1996.

3 Read and Think

Step 1. **Work with a group. What do you put on résumés? What do you know about job applications? Make a word map like the one below. (The one below is just an example.)**

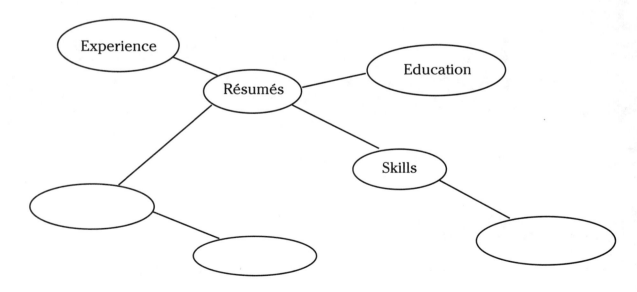

Step 2. Theo's looking for a job. Read his résumé.

Theo Wolinski
485 Mann Blvd.
Torrance, CA
(310) 874-2467

Work Experience

1992–1996	Warehouse Manager Simco Industries, Los Angeles Managed the warehouse, with a staff of thirty people and two shifts
1991–1992	Technician, Simco Industries, Los Angeles, CA Was responsible for maintenance of equipment and electrical work
1987–1991	Chief Electrician/Manager State Telephone and Communications Company, Warsaw, Poland Managed staff of technicians and electricians at state-owned telecommunications company
1982–1987	Electrician State Telephone and Communications Company, Warsaw, Poland Worked as electrician at state-owned telecommunications company

Education

1982	Graduate, State Technical Institute, Warsaw. Specialization: Electronics

Skills:
Management and leadership skills
Specialization in electrical work
Equipment maintenance
Mechanics

Step 3. Read the vocabulary below. Then read Theo's résumé again.

Step 4. With your group, discuss this question: How did Theo organize his résumé?

Vocabulary

be responsible for to have specific job duties: a waiter is responsible for serving customers in a restaurant

shifts times of work (during the day, in the evening, at night)

maintenance keeping things in good condition and working order

telecommunications communication by telephone and other similar means

Practice

Choose the correct word for each of the following sentences.

welder   welding helmet   manager   electrician   résumé

1. A ___*welder*___ has to protect his or her eyes from the light of the welding torch.

2. According to company rules, every welder must wear a _____ when he or she is working.

3. Jorge sent his _____ to every company in his city, but he is still waiting for a reply.

4. Bruce called the _____ of the bank to ask for a job.

5. The _____ installed the wiring yesterday, so now we have lighting.

6. Put on your _____ before you start that job.

7. When you write your _____, put down all of your experience.

4 Put It in Writing

Step 1. On a separate sheet of paper, list your education. List schools, certificates, and diplomas.

Step 2. On a second sheet of paper, list your skills.

Step 3. On a third sheet of paper, list your job experience. (Write a job objective if you have never worked.)

Step 4. Create a timeline. Put your job experience on the timeline, along with dates. Use Theo's timeline as a model.

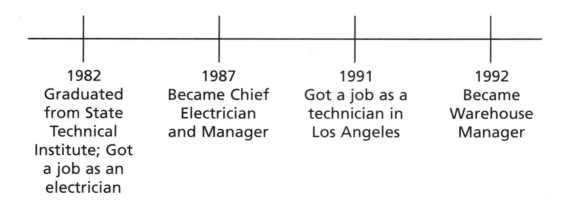

1982
Graduated
from State
Technical
Institute; Got
a job as an
electrician

1987
Became Chief
Electrician
and Manager

1991
Got a job as a
technician in
Los Angeles

1992
Became
Warehouse
Manager

Put your own information on the timeline below.

_____

Step 5. On a fourth sheet of paper, create a single list. Put your job experience first, and put your most recent job first. Put your education after your job experience, and put your skills last. (If you have no job experience, list a job objective or goal.)

Step 6. With a partner, compare your work. Save your papers for later.

5 Listen and Speak

Step 1. Listen to the conversation. Two people are talking about résumés.

A: Would you like some help with your résumé?
B: That would be great. I am having some trouble.
A: This is interesting. But why did you start with your first job?
B: Well, I prefer to put things in chronological order.
A: That's good, but you should start with your most recent job.
B: Maybe, but they laid me off from my most recent job.
A: Really? That's terrible!
B: Yeah. They laid off a hundred people at the same time. We were all working overtime one evening when the boss came in and announced it.
A: That's awful. But I still think you should list your most recent job first. It won't hurt you. Layoffs are very common, and it's not your fault.

Step 2. Practice the conversation with a partner.

Step 3. With your partner, talk about the lists you made. What were your problems? Discuss the problems you had and why.

Step 4. Brainstorm some ideas for improvement of your work.

6 Read and Write

Step 1. Read Johnna's résumé. Johnna listed her job duties under each job.

Johnna McGlaughlin
398 Allen St.
Milwaukee, WI

Teaching Experience

1994–Present   Community Education Instructor, District 78
Helped ESL students to acquire and develop writing skills

1991–1994   Peace Corps Volunteer
Taught English in Malaysia

1986–1991   Teacher at Glendalough Secondary School, Dublin, Ireland
Taught English literature and composition
Graded exams and participated in professional conferences

1981–1986   Sales Clerk, McGarrity's Supermarket, Dublin, Ireland

Writing Skills

Writer of lesson outlines, curriculum objectives, reports
Writer of test passages for the Educational Testing Service

Computer Skills

PC skills: word processing, knowledge of all major word-processing programs

---

Step 2. Answer the questions.

1. In what country did Johnna work in 1992? _Malaysia._____

2. What did Johnna do in 1992? _____

3. What was Johnna's second job? _____

4. What does Johnna have the most experience at? _____

5. What skills does Johnna have? _____

6. What was Johnna's most recent job? _____

Step 3. With a partner, compare your answers.

Form and Function

1 A: Do you mind if I show you my résumé?
   B: Not at all.

Question:	**Do you mind if**	I, we, they	**do** that?
		he, she, it	**does** that?
Answer:	(It's OK.)	(It's not OK.)	
	No, not at all.	**Yes, I do.**	
	No, I don't mind.	**Yes, I mind.**	
	Sure. Go ahead.		

Examples

A: **Do you mind if** I **smoke?** B: No, go ahead. OR: **Yes, I mind.** We don't like smoke in here.
A: **Do you mind if** I **ask** you a question? B: **Not at all.** What is it? OR: **Sorry. I don't have time.**
A: **Do you mind if** I **finish** this tomorrow? B: **No. That's all right.** OR: **Well, yes,** we're in a hurry.
We need it today.

Practice 1

A. Listen to the questions and answers and mark OK or Not OK for the answers.

1.(OK)   Not OK   **3.** OK   Not OK   **5.** OK   Not OK

2. OK   Not OK   **4.** OK   Not OK   **6.** OK   Not OK

B. On a separate sheet of paper, write answers for the questions below. Follow the responses in parentheses.

1. Do you mind if I leave early?   (That's not OK.)
2. Do you mind if I ask you a question?   (That's OK.)
3. Do you mind if I take next week off?   (That's not OK.)
4. Do you mind if I sit down?   (That's OK.)

C. Talk to a partner. Ask if he/she minds if you do the following:

- smoke
- tell (him/her) a story
- ask a personal question
- talk to (him/her) after class
- borrow a dollar from (him/her)
- show (him/her) pictures of your family

- other: _____

2 I prefer to put things in chronological order.

	I, you, we, they he, she, (it)	**prefer to** **prefers to**	do it this way.	
What do **does**	I, you, we, they he, she, it	**prefer to**	do?	
Do **Does**	you he, she	**want to**	do that?	Yes, **I do.** / No, **I don't.** Yes, he, she **does.** No, he, she **doesn't.**

Examples

I **prefer to** work in the evening. In the morning, I **prefer to** sleep.
Harvey **needs to** get more exercise. He spends his whole day at a desk.
Julia **wants to** find a new job, but she **doesn't want to** work as a secretary anymore.
What kind of work **do** you **like to** do?

Practice 2

A. Listen and circle the words you hear.

1. (likes to)   likes   **3.** needs to   needs   **5.** prefers to   prefers

2. prefers to   prefers   **4.** want to   want   **6.** wants to   wants

B. Complete each sentence with the correct choice from the pair in parentheses.

1. I _____*like to*_____ (like/like to) work in groups with other employees.

2. However, Sheila _____ (prefers/prefers to) work by herself.

3. A: Which do you like better, daytime hours or nighttime hours?

     B: I _____ (prefer/prefer to) daytime hours.

4. We _____ (need/need to) more information about the kinds of jobs available
in this area.

**C. Talk to a partner. Discuss these questions: Do you prefer to work for a company or to start
your own business? Do you prefer to work in the morning or in the evening? Do you prefer
to work in the city, the suburbs, or the country?**

3 Would you like some help with your résumé?

	Noun			Verb
Would you like	some <u>help</u>?		**Would you like**	<u>to fill out</u> an application?
Yes, **I would.** /No, **I wouldn't.**				

Examples

A: **Would you like** a cup of coffee? B: Thank you. That would be nice.
Would you like a hand with that? **Would you like** some help with that?

Practice 3

A. Listen and circle the words you hear.

1. (would)   did   3. would   did   5. would   did

2. would   did   4. would   did   6. would   did

B. Think of three things to offer a partner. Write three sentences with *Would you like . . . ?*

Example: _Would you like some help with that exercise?_____

1. _____

2. _____

3. _____

C. Now talk to a partner. Choose one of the offers you wrote in Activity B. Ask your partner a question with *Would you like . . . ?*

4 We were all working overtime one evening when the boss announced the news.

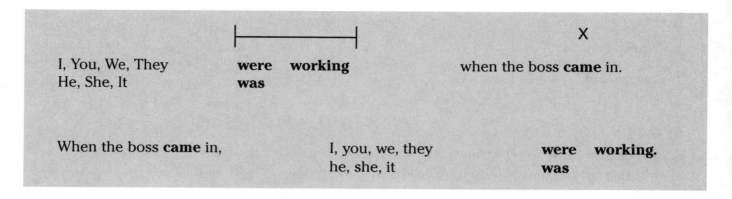

Examples

When the electricity **went** out, we **were trying** to fix a serious computer problem.
I **was walking** down the hallway when Allen **tripped** and **spilled** coffee on me.

Practice 4

A. Listen and circle the words you hear. Then decide if the action is the longer or shorter of the two for each sentence.

1. worked (working) (longer) shorter   3. walked   walking   longer   shorter

2. dialed   dialing   longer   shorter   4. typed   typing   longer   shorter

B. What were you doing when class started today? What were you doing when your plane arrived in the United States? What were you doing when you met your wife/husband? What were you doing when . . .? Answer these questions or any other questions of your own below. Write three sentences.

Example: *I was talking to Irina when class started today.*

1. _____

2. _____

3. _____

C. With a partner, compare your sentences. Talk about what you were doing and when.

Putting It to Work

1 Pair Work

Step 1. Listen as Jorge describes his work experience. Take notes and complete the timeline.

_____

Step 2. With a partner, ask questions about Jorge's work experience to compare your timelines. List Jorge's work experience chronologically.

Example:
A: What did Jorge do in 1978?
B: He worked as an electrician in Colombia.

2 Pair Work

Step 1. With a partner, reread your lists of skills and education from the writing activity on page 30. On a separate sheet of paper, write the heading for your résumé. Write your name, address, and telephone number at the top. Use this model:

Jorge Sanchez
4583 South Shore Boulevard
Chicago, IL 60698
Telephone: (312) 845-9457

Step 2. Copy your work experience and education from your list. Leave extra space after each job. (If you have no work experience, write a job objective.) For each job, you can list your job duties, and if you wish, you can list your job skills.

Example: 1986–1990   Restaurant Manager

- Managed a large Korean restaurant   **Job Duties**
- Supervised and scheduled 30 employees
- Purchased supplies and hired new employees

Ability to supervise and manage large restaurant operation   **Job Skills**
Thorough knowledge of restaurant suppliers
Good budgeting and financial skills

Step 3. Look at your partner's résumé and critique it. Is the work experience arranged chronologically? Do the job titles have explanations of job duties? Did your partner list his or her skills? Did your partner list his or her education? Give your partner some suggestions.

Step 4. Take notes on your partner's suggestions and think about them. Should you change your résumé?

3 Group/Class Work

Step 1. Form a group and choose a team leader, a team recorder, and a team reporter. Choose one of the timelines from among your group members' work or use the timeline in this unit.

Step 2. Choose an occupation and write a job objective.

Step 3. List skills and experience for this occupation in a chart like the one below.

Skills	Experience

Step 4. Write a fictional history of work experience and education for this occupation. Follow the model of the résumés on pages 29 and 32.

Step 5. Your team reporter will go to the board and copy your job history on the board.

Step 6. Look at your classmates' job histories on the board. What can you improve? What can you add?

4 Culture Work

In the United States, many employers value the following characteristics in employees:

Willingness to take initiative
Willingness to take responsibility for one's work

Look at the pictures below and discuss the situations.

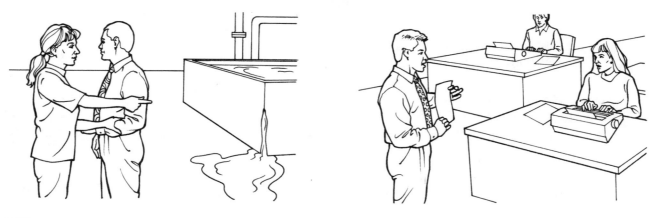

Unit 4
INTERVIEWS AND APPLYING FOR JOBS

Openers

Look at the picture and the application form. Match the categories below to the correct section on the form in the picture.

address   education   experience

248 S. Edgewood Place
Covina, CA

Covina High School   9/87-6/91
Covina, CA

Marker's Restaurant   waitress 1/91-5/97
Covina, CA

Alma is applying for a job. She has an interview. Jorge is after Alma. Have you ever been in this situation? Where?

1 Listen and Think

Listen to the interview. Then answer the questions with a partner.

1. What position is Jorge applying for?

2. Are there any openings for that position? If so, how many?

3. Is Jorge working now? If so, what is he doing?

4. Which shift does Jorge want to work? Why?

5. Did Jorge get the job?

2 Talk to a Partner

Step 1.   Practice the conversation with a partner.

A: Hello, I'm John Cranston. Help yourself to some coffee
and have a seat.

B: Thank you, Mr. Cranston.

A: We have several applicants for the sales clerk position.
Tell me about your work experience.

B: I worked as a sales clerk at Bargain City for two years,
and before that I was a sales clerk and a stocker
at Shop-Mart.

A: You must like this kind of work, then.

B: Yes, I do. But I would be interested in the warehouse job, too.

A: All right. I'll keep you in mind for both positions, and I'll let you
know one way or another by next week.

B: Thank you. It was very nice meeting you.

**Step 2.   With the same partner, use the information below or use your own information to
have a conversation like this one. Change roles.**

Position desired:	Truck driver		
Work experience:	Truck driver	Acme Trucking	1988–1993
	Truck driver	Dawson Delivery	1985–1988
Position desired:	Electrician		
Work experience:	Electrician	Star Lighting	1994–1995
	Electrician	Weber Electrical	1989–1994

3 Read and Think

Step 1.   Read the text below.

Juan Cortez is a supervisor in the shipping department at Fairview Hospital Supplies, Inc. He
needs to hire a new shipping clerk, and he has received two applications for the position.
He wants to hire someone with experience as a shipping clerk and preferably someone who
has worked in a metal products company. The person he hires must have at least a high school
education.

Step 2. With a partner, look at the two applications below. Which applicant should Mr. Cortez hire? Does either applicant meet all of Mr. Cortez's requirements?

Fairview Hospital Supplies, Inc.
APPLICATION FOR EMPLOYMENT

Last Name: Rodriguez
First Name: Salvatore
Social Security No.: 545-99-8897
Position Desired: Shipping clerk

Present/Previous Employers
Company: Safeguard Plastics
City/State: Dominguez Hills, CA
Type of Business: Plastic products
Job(s) Held: Plastic molder
Dates: 5/94 - present
Reason for leaving: Still employed

Company: Switzer Aluminum
City/State: Carson, CA
Type of Business: Aluminum products
Job(s) Held: Janitor; shipping clerk
Dates: Janitor - 4/82–7/85;
                  Shipping clerk -7/85–5/94
Reason for leaving: Higher salary

Education/Training
School: Compton Community College
City/State: Compton, CA
Course of Study: Computer Programming
Dates Attended: 9/95–12/95
Degree/Certificate
awarded: None - only took one class

Fairview Hospital Supplies, Inc.
APPLICATION FOR EMPLOYMENT

Last Name: Jackson
First Name: Clinton
Social Security No.: 438-22-3476
Position Desired: Shipping clerk

Present/Previous Employers
Company: Bolton Manufacturing
City/State: Tucson, AZ
Type of Business: Auto parts manufacturing
Job(s) Held: Shipping clerk
Dates: 4/91–9/95
Reason for leaving: Moved to California

Education/Training
School: Catalina High School
City/State: Tucson, AZ
Course of Study: General
Dates Attended: 9/88–3/91
Degree/Certificate
awarded: None - did not finish

Vocabulary

applicant a person applying for a job
position desired the job the applicant wants
preferably not required but strongly desired
at least a minimum amount
hire give a job to someone
job requirements qualities that an applicant needs to get the job
previous employers employers that an applicant had in the past

Practice

Complete the sentences with the correct words from the vocabulary list on page 41.

1. I don't think I meet all of their ____*job requirements*____. I don't know how to type and I don't have computer experience.

2. My supervisor is going to hire a new clerk, _____ someone with experience.

3. Maria just arrived in the United States so all of her _____ are located in Mexico.

4. Ernie is looking for a new job. He wants to make _____ $7.50 an hour.

5. I doubt that I'll get an interview for that job. The human resources office told me there are twenty

   other _____ for the position.

4 Put It in Writing

Step 1. **Look again at the two applications for the job in Mr. Cortez's department. Imagine that you are Mr. Cortez and you are going to interview these applicants. Write three questions to ask each applicant in order to get more information.**

Example: _____*Do you have experience with computers?*_____

Questions for Salvatore Rodriguez:

1. _____

2. _____

3. _____

Questions for Clinton Jackson:

1. _____

2. _____

3. _____

Step 2. **Compare your questions with a partner. Put all of your questions together and then write any additional questions you might need to conduct a complete interview of each applicant.**

5 Listen and Speak

Step 1. A job applicant is having an interview. Listen to the conversation.

A: Your retail sales experience is good, but tell me,
have you ever sold cameras or computer equipment?

B: Yes, I've sold cameras. But I haven't sold any computer equipment.

A: Here, all our cash registers are computerized. For each sale, we read
the price with a bar code scanner. Have you ever used anything like that?

B: Yes, I have. Actually I've used bar code scanners quite a lot.

A: That's good. So you've used computerized cash registers, then, too?

B: Yes. In fact, I've never used any other kind of cash register. And I know
how to use personal computers, too.

A: That's good. That was my next question, because we keep a list of our
customers in a data base. Have you ever used a data base?

B: No, I haven't. But I'm sure I could learn.

Step 2. Practice the conversation with a partner.

**Step 3. With your partner, role-play a similar conversation about one of the following jobs
and skills.**

Job	Skills	Other Requirements
Truck driver	Drive a tractor-trailer; do heavy lifting, loading, unloading	Have a license to drive a truck
Word processor/typist	Use a computer; use word-processing software	Type 55 words per minute
Nurse	Take care of patients; give injections; take patients' blood pressure	Have a nursing certificate
Other		

**Step 4. Find another pair of classmates and form a group. Choose a team leader, a team
recorder, and a team reporter. Choose any job you know. Talk about the skills and
experience necessary. Your team recorder will take notes.**

**Step 5. For this job, brainstorm a list of interview questions. What would an interviewer
ask? Then think of answers to the interviewer's questions.**

Step 6. Role-play the interview in your group.

Step 7. Your team leader and your team reporter will role-play the interview for the class.

6 Read and Write

Step 1. Read the portion of résumé below. Then fill out the employment history section of the application with the information provided in the résumé.

Vu Nguyen
4920 E. 24th Street
Camarillo, CA 93265
(805) 578-1244

Work Experience

1993–present	Packer, FreshFarm Foods, Camarillo, CA. Responsibilities include packing and inventory control. Occasional forklift driving.
1990–1993	Stocker, Jones Foods, Camarillo, CA. Was responsible for stocking shelves, checking prices, and taking inventory. Promoted from bagger position after six months on the job.
1989–1990	Bagger, Jones Foods, Camarillo, CA. Bagged groceries at check-out stand, and assisted customers to their cars on request.

EMPLOYMENT HISTORY

Please list previous employers. List most recent employer first. Attach additional sheet if necessary.
MAY WE CONTACT YOUR PRESENT EMPLOYER? ☐ YES ☐ NO

COMPANY		SUPERVISOR	
STARTING SALARY $	ENDING $	MONTH YEAR FROM	MONTH YEAR TO
PHONE NUMBER		TITLE OF POSITION AND DUTIES PERFORMED	
STREET ADDRESS			
CITY STATE ZIP		REASON FOR LEAVING	
COMPANY		SUPERVISOR	
STARTING SALARY $	ENDING $	MONTH YEAR FROM	MONTH YEAR TO
PHONE NUMBER		TITLE OF POSITION AND DUTIES PERFORMED	
STREET ADDRESS			
CITY STATE ZIP		REASON FOR LEAVING	

Step 2. Write a list of the information that is not included in the résumé that you still need to complete the application.

Step 3. With a classmate, compare your lists.

Form and Function

1 You must like this kind of work.

| I, you, he, she, we, they | **must** | like this work. |

Examples

George has lunch with Carol every day. He **must** like her.

Flavio went back to Brazil three times this year. He **must** still have family there.

Practice 1

A. Listen to the dialogues. Circle the response you hear.

1. You're excited.   (You must be excited.)

2. She's sick.   She must be sick.

3. He must have a lot of money.   He has a lot of money.

4. We're late.   We must be late.

B. Write a response to each of the statements below using *must* and any words in parentheses.

Example: A: I just got a raise!   B: (you) (work) **You must work** hard.

1. A: I heard Sam and Phil quit.

   B: (they) (have) ___*They must have*___ other jobs.

2. A: The lights are off at the store.

   B: (it) (be) _____ closed.

3. A: Who's that woman over there?

   B: (she) (be) _____ our new supervisor.

4. A: Why do we have to come in early tomorrow?

   B: (we) (have) _____ a meeting with the boss.

5. A: I'll be gone for three weeks.

   B: (you) (have) _____ a lot of vacation time.

2 A: Where are you going on vacation?
   B: I'm not sure yet. I might go to San Francisco.

I, you, he, she, it, we, they	**might** go to . . .
I, you, he, she, it, we, they	**might not** go to . . .

Examples

Paul doesn't feel well; he **might** call in sick tomorrow. He **might not** be able to finish his shift today either. Susana and David aren't sure if they can come to class tonight. They **might** have to work late.

Practice 2

A. Listen. For each statement, circle Yes if the speaker talks about something definite; circle Maybe if the speaker talks about a possibility.

1. Yes	Maybe	3. Yes	Maybe	5. Yes	Maybe
2. Yes	Maybe	4. Yes	Maybe	6. Yes	Maybe

B. Think of three things you might do on your next vacation. Write them on a separate sheet of paper. Then tell a partner.

3 A: Have you ever sold cameras or computer equipment?
   B: Yes, I've sold cameras, but I haven't sold computer equipment.

Have	I, you, we, they		ever	work**ed**?
Has	he, she, it		ever	work**ed**?
Yes,	I, you, we, they	**have.**		
No,	I, you, we, they	**haven't.**		
Yes,	he, she, it	**has.**		
No,	he, she, it	**hasn't.**		
I, you, we, they		**have**	never	**had** . . .
he, she, it		**has**	never	**had** . . .

Examples

A: **Has** Sam **ever been** late for work? B: No, he **hasn't.** He **has never been** sick either.
A: **Have** we **ever met** the new supervisor? B: Yes, we **have.**
A: **Has** she **ever worked** with us? B: No, she **hasn't.** She **has never worked** in our department.

Practice 3

A. Listen. Circle the correct answer.

1. a. work   (worked)
    b. haven't have

2. a. has   have
    b. has   have

3. a. talked   talk
    b. hasn't   has

B. Write a question after each statement using the correct form of the words in parentheses.

Example: José has never had a full-time job.
(you) (ever) (work) **Have you ever worked** full time?

1. I have never been to Guatemala. (Jerry) (ever) (visit) _Has Jerry ever visited_ Guatemala?

2. No one in this department has ever run this machine. (anyone) (ever) (use)

_____ a machine like it?

3. We have never told the company president about this problem.

(our supervisor) (ever) (speak) _____ to him?

4. You have never been to my house. (you) (ever) (go) _____ to Dora's apartment?

C. Work with a partner. Find the answer to these questions: Have the people in the chart below ever done the activities in the chart? Complete the chart with your partner's information. Student A: Look at this page only. Student B: Look at page 48.

Example:
B: Has Ted ever worked with computers?
A: Yes, he has. He's worked with computers a lot.

	Worked with computers?	Operated a cash register?	Used a fax machine?
Ted	Yes. A lot.	No. Never.	Yes. Once or twice.
Bob			
Alice	No. Never.	Yes. A few times.	Yes. Once or twice.
Mary			
Your partner			

Work with a partner. Find the answer to these questions: Have the people in the chart below ever done the activities in the chart? Complete the chart with your partner's information. Student B: Look at this page only. Student A: Look at page 47.

Example:

A: Has Bob ever worked with computers?

B: No, he hasn't. He's never worked with computers.

	Worked with computers?	Operated a cash register?	Used a fax machine?
Ted			
Bob	No. Never.	Yes. A lot.	No. Never.
Alice			
Mary	Yes. A lot.	Yes. A few times.	Yes. A few times.
Your partner			

D. Now, on a separate sheet of paper, write a paragraph about the people in the chart. Start your paragraph with this sentence:

I have looked at the skills and experience of several people and have found the following results.

E. Exchange papers with your partner for Activity D. Correct your partner's paper and then look at your partner's corrections to your paper. Discuss your corrections.

F. Role-play.

Student A: You are interviewing for a job as a supervisor. Describe your work experience and previous job responsibilities to the interviewer. Tell him/her why you think you are qualified for the job.

Student B: You are a manager interviewing someone to supervise one of your departments. Be sure to get as much information as you can about this candidate. Explain to him/her what the qualifications and responsibilities are for this position.

Change roles and interview for a different type of job.

Putting It to Work

1 Pair Work

Step 1. Listen to an employer interviewing two applicants for the same job. Rate the two applicants on the following qualities:

Quality	Excellent	Good	Fair	Poor
Politeness				
Professionalism				
Enthusiasm				
Ability to explain				
Self-confidence				

Step 2. Compare your ratings with a partner. How important do you think these qualities are in an interview? Do you think it is fair to rate an applicant on these qualities or are work experience and education the only factors to consider? Discuss your opinion with your partner.

2 Pair Work

Toward the end of an interview, the employer usually gives the applicant an opportunity to ask questions too. This allows the applicant to get more information about the job he/she is applying for, but it also shows how interested the applicant is in getting the job. If an applicant does not ask any questions, the employer might think he/she isn't very interested in the job.

Step 1. Think about the interviews you heard for the accounting clerk position above. With your partner, think of questions the applicant could ask the employer in that situation. Write a list of questions.

Step 2. Role-play. Continue the interview for the accounting clerk position.

Student A: You are the employer and you are very interested in this applicant. You want to give him/her lots of information so that he/she will consider taking the job.

Student B: You are the applicant from the first interview above. You are very interested in the position, and you want to know as much as possible about the position.

3 Group/Class Work

Step 1. Form a group of three to four students. Choose a team leader, a team recorder, and a team reporter. Choose one of the want ads from Unit 1 and write a list of interview questions for applicants for the position.

Step 2. When you are ready to begin interviewing, give your ad to another group.

Step 3. For the ad your group received from another group, work together to brainstorm questions the applicant might ask the interviewer about the position.

Step 4. Your team reporter will role-play the interview for your ad in front of the class.

4 Culture Work

Read the situations below and discuss the questions with the class.

1. Myrna Carillo answered a want ad and filled out an application for a secretarial position at a college. She waited about two weeks and did not hear from the personnel office, so she called the company.

Myrna: Hi. My name's Myrna Carillo. I applied for a secretarial position about two weeks ago, but I haven't heard from you. Could you please tell me whether you plan to interview for that position soon?
Personnel: Hold on just a minute and let me check. Oh, I'm sorry but that position has already been filled.
Myrna: Oh. Well, thank you anyway.

Do you think Myrna was justified in calling the personnel office? Would this be appropriate in your native country? If not, what would you do differently in your native country? Discuss this with the class.

2. Fred Parker was interviewed for a job as a quality control inspector at a large factory. The company's vice-president and one of the engineers conducted the interview. They told Fred that it would probably take a week for them to finish all the interviews and make their decision.

The day after the interview, Fred wrote thank-you letters to the vice-president and the engineer who interviewed him. He thanked them for the opportunity to meet them and discuss his qualifications, and he expressed a great deal of interest in their company.

Why do you think Fred wrote the thank-you letters? Do you think that was an appropriate thing for him to do? Would it be appropriate in your native country? Discuss this with the class.

Unit 5
PAYCHECKS AND DEDUCTIONS

Openers

Look at the pay stub and identify the following:

deductions (money held back)   employee   pay period (dates)
net pay (take-home pay)   employer   pay rate (pay per hour)

(A) HAMILTON/HARTMAN HOSPITALITY, INC.

Earnings Statement

FROM: 01-14-96 **(B)**
TO: 01-27-96

(C) Teresa M. Lopez
      2704 W. Southwood
      North Rock, TX 51234

SSN: 123-45-6789
Tax Status: SINGLE
Allowances: 3

EARNINGS	rate	hours	this period	year-to-date
Regular	**(D)** 6.75	80.0	540.00	1,080.00
O.T.	10.13	8.0	81.04	202.60
GROSS PAY			621.04	1,282.60
DEDUCTIONS				
Federal Income Tax			44.19	91.05
(E) FICA			47.50	125.16
Med. Insur. (Family)			101.95	203.90
TTL DEDUCTIONS			193.64	447.11
NET PAY			427.40	835.49
			(F)	

How often does this employee get paid? How often do you get paid? In Texas, there is no state income tax. Where you live, is there a state income tax?

1 Listen and Think

Listen and answer the questions with a partner.

1. Is Federal income tax a required deduction for Teresa?

2. Is medical insurance a required deduction for her?

3. How much does Teresa's employer contribute to her medical insurance?

2 Talk to a Partner

Step 1. Practice the conversation with a partner.

A: So, how much do they take out of your check?
B: Well, let me see. Last time, it was 165 dollars.
A: How much was that?
    I mean, what percent?
B: Let me figure it out.
    OK, well, it's about 20 percent.
A: Hmm. I guess everyone is different.

GROSS PAY:	625.00
DEDUCTIONS:	(this period)
Fed. Inc. Tax.	52.38
FICA	54.27
Hosp. Ins.	55.85
401-K	25.00
TOTAL DEDUCTIONS:	187.50

Step 2. Now, with the same partner, practice the conversation using the information above. Figure the percentage of deductions that this worker pays.

Step 3. Practice the conversation with the information from your own paycheck.

3 Read and Think

Step 1. Read and answer the questions below with a partner. They will prepare you to understand Form W-4.

1. Are you **married**? If Yes,
    (a) does your husband or wife live in the United States?
    (b) do you complete your income tax together with your spouse?
    (c) does your spouse work in the United States?
2. Do you have **more than one job**? If Yes, do you earn
    (a) more than $1,000 per year from your second job, or
    (b) less than $1,000 per year from your second job?
3. Do you have any **dependents**? This means a spouse, children, or other family members who live with you and whom you support (housing, food, clothing, etc.).

Step 2. Read the instructions for Form W-4.

Form W-4 (1996)

Purpose. Complete Form W-4 so that your employer can withhold the correct amount of Federal income tax from your pay.

Basic Instructions. Employees should complete the Personal Allowances Worksheet.

Head of Household. Generally, you may claim to be a "head of household" only if you are (a) unmarried, (b) have dependents living with you, and (c) pay more than 50% of the living costs for yourself and your dependents.

Step 3. With your partner, read the Personal Allowances Worksheet for Form W-4.

Personal Allowances Worksheet

A Enter "1" for **yourself** if no one else can claim you as a dependent . . . . **A** _____

B Enter "1" if:
- You are single and have only one job; or
- You are married, have only one job, and your spouse does not work; or
- Your wages from a second job or your spouse's wages (or the total of both) are $1,000 or less.

. . **B** _____

C Enter "1" for your **spouse**. But, you may choose to enter -0- if you are married and have either a working spouse or more than one job (this may help you avoid having too little tax withheld) . . . . **C** _____

D Enter number of **dependents** (other than your spouse or yourself) you will claim on your tax return . . . . **D** _____

E Enter "1" if you will file as **head of household** on your tax return (see conditions under **Head of Household** above) . **E** _____

F Enter "1" if you have at least $1,500 of **child or dependent care expenses** for which you plan to claim a credit . . **F** _____

G Add lines A through F and enter total here. **Note:** This amount may be different from the number of exemptions you claim on your return ▶ **G** _____

For accuracy, do all worksheets that apply.
- If you plan to **itemize or claim adjustments to income** and want to reduce your withholding, see the Deductions and Adjustments Worksheet on page 2.
- If you are **single** and have **more than one job** and your combined earnings from all jobs exceed $30,000 OR if you are **married** and have a **working spouse or more than one job,** and the combined earnings from all jobs exceed $50,000, see the Two-Earner/Two-Job Worksheet on page 2 if you want to avoid having too little tax withheld.
- If **neither** of the above situations applies, **stop here** and enter the number from line G on line 5 of Form W-4 below.

Step 4. With a partner, figure how many allowances these people should put on their Form W-4. Use the information above, especially the "Personal Allowances."

- **PERSON X** A married man with a wife and three children. He works one full-time job. His wife takes care of the children and does not work outside the home. How many allowances should he claim on his W-4?   _____

- **PERSON Y** A divorced woman with two children. She works full-time. She gets some money from her ex-husband to help support the children, but not much and not every month. She has to pay $300 a month for day care and asks for a tax credit for that.   _____

- **PERSON Z** A married man whose wife and four children live in his native country. He regularly sends them money. They have social security numbers and he claims them as dependents on his income tax forms.   _____

Step 5. Read the vocabulary below and then read the instructions for Form W-4 again.

Vocabulary

allowance that which is permitted
taxes money paid to the government
claim (to)/(a) request, ask for
dependent a person who depends on
someone else for financial support

expenses costs that you have to pay
head the leader or main person; examples: head
of a department, a household, a political party
spouse someone's husband or wife

Practice

Look at the groups of actions below. In each group, put the actions into the correct order, based on how these steps usually happen. Write 1 for the first step in each group and 5 for the last action in the sequence.

GROUP A	GROUP B
PAYCHECKS	TAXES
_____ Your company's Payroll/Personnel office figures out how much to deduct from your check.	_____ You fill out your Income Tax Return before April 15th every year.
_____ You earn your pay based on your wages and the hours you work (or other payment system).	_____ You fill out one or two W-4 forms (Federal and state—if your state has an income tax). You give it to your employer so the employer knows how much money to withhold for taxes.
_____ You get hired for a job, and you find out your work schedule and how much they will pay you.	_____ You check your paycheck to see if your employer is taking out the right amount of taxes.
_____ Your company (usually the Payroll/Personnel office) asks about your deductions (your allowances on the W-4 and what you choose like medical insurance).	_____ Your employer withholds taxes from your paycheck every pay period and lists them on your pay stub.
_____ You get your paycheck with its pay stub. You check it to make sure it is right and that you understand.	_____ Every year in January, your employer gives you a report (W-2 form) about how much you earned and how much tax your employer withheld.

With a partner, compare your answers.

4 Put It in Writing

Step 1. Select Group A or Group B from page 54. Write the steps in order in a paragraph. Use "my" instead of "your."

Step 2. Compare your answers with a partner who wrote for the same Group ("A" with "A"). Check with the teacher if you are not sure or cannot agree.

Step 3. Now read your paragraphs aloud to a new partner who wrote for the other Group ("A" with "B"). And listen to that partner's paragraph, too.

5 Listen and Speak

Step 1. Listen to the conversation.

A: Excuse me, do you mind if I ask you a question about my paycheck?

B: Sure, go ahead.

A: I don't understand something here. My paycheck was bigger last time. And Carlos had the highest take-home pay. But his gross pay is lower than mine.

B: How much was your paycheck last time?

A: Four hundred and fifty dollars.

B: How much is it this time?

A: Four hundred and thirty.

B: Hmm. That's a difference of twenty dollars. How many hours did you work?

A: The same as last time—forty.

B: Oh, I know why. You decided to take only one allowance, remember?

A: Yes, I remember. So I should get more money, not less.

B: No, it doesn't work like that. When you have more allowances, you get more money.

A: Oh, then I should change that. I should take more allowances, not fewer.

B: Well, how many children do you have?

A: Two.

B: Then you can take three allowances at most.

Step 2. Practice the conversation with a partner.

Step 3. With your partner, look at your own paycheck, or look at the pay stub on page 51. Figure the percentage of deductions for the pay stub. Is there a way to receive more take-home pay?

Step 4. With your partner, discuss the following: If you take more allowances, you receive more money in your paycheck, but you have a higher tax bill at the end of the year. If your tax bill is too high, sometimes you have to pay a penalty. Do you prefer to make more money now or pay less tax at the end of the year?

6 Read and Write

Step 1. Read the section below from the Employee Handbook for Fairview Hospital Supplies, In

Section 9. Payroll Deductions.

After your gross pay is calculated for each pay period, the Personnel/Payroll Office will figure your <u>payroll deductions</u>.

There are several types of payroll deductions. Some are required by law. Others depend on your individual situation, the personal choices that you make, or the position that you have within the company.

A. Mandatory deductions/withholding taxes required by law.

(The same level for everyone.)
1. Social Security Tax = 6.25 %
2. Medicare Tax = 1.45 %

(Depending on individual factors.)
3. Federal Income Tax—depends on allowances claimed on Form W-4
4. State Income Tax—also depends on allowances claimed

B. Voluntary deductions.

1. Medical Insurance—according to the plan you select (if any)
2. Dental Insurance—according to the plan you select (if any)
3. 401-K/Retirement Savings—the amount you select to save (if any)
4. Crusade of Mercy Contributions—the amount you select (recommended)

C. Position-based deductions.

1. Union Dues—if applicable
2. Uniform Fee—if applicable
3. Credit Union Savings—the amount you want to deposit to your account
   (hourly employees only)

The type, dollar amount, and total amount of all payroll deductions are clearly indicated on every paycheck stub.

If you have any questions, if your situation changes, or if you wish to change your voluntary deductions, notify the Personnel/Payroll Office in person during regular office hours or in writing. NOTE: Some changes may take up to one month to go into effect.

Step 2. Write short lists of the following payroll deductions: (*a*) deductions every worker has, (*b*) deductions only some workers have, and (*c*) deductions you take only if you want to. Refer to your own paycheck as a reference.

Step 3. In groups, compare your answers. Discuss your answers with the rest of the class also.

Form and Function

1 A: I don't understand this. My paycheck was bigger last time.
B: That's because you decided to take only one allowance.

My paycheck was	bigger	last time.
It was	bigger	**than** this time.
		than it is now.

good	>	**better**	big	>	**bigger**	easy	>	eas**ier**
bad	>	**worse**	fat	>	fatter	happy	>	happ**ier**
			thin	>	thin**ner**	heavy	>	heav**ier**

difficult	(diff i cult)	>	**more** difficult
interesting	(in te rest ing)	>	**more** interesting

Examples

Last month I worked **more overtime**, so I had a **bigger** paycheck **than** the month before.
Carlos worked **less**, so his check was **smaller**.

Practice 1

A. Listen and circle the words you hear.

1. big ⬭bigger⬮   **3.** difficult   more difficult   **5.** high   higher

2. small   smaller   **4.** easy   easier   **6.** low   lower

B. Complete the sentences with the correct forms from among the choices in parentheses.

Rita worked 50 hours, with 10 hours of overtime, so her paycheck was really (high, higher)

_____*high*_____. Other people worked less overtime, so their paychecks were

(low, lower) _____ than Rita's. Some of the employees feel that is unfair.
They make a salary, and their paychecks are always the same. Sometimes, some of them have a

(small, smaller) _____ paycheck than Rita, and sometimes they have a

(big, bigger) _____ one.

2 Carlos had the highest take-home pay.

better	**best**	bigger	big**gest**		eas**ier**	easi**est**
worse	**worst**	fatter	fat**test**		happ**ier**	happi**est**
		thinner	thin**nest**		heav**ier**	heav**iest**
		more difficult	**most** difficult			
		more interesting	**most** interesting			

Examples

Employees in government jobs often have **the best** benefits. Newer employees in small, private sector companies are **least likely** to have benefits. The **most typical** benefit among full-time workers (66 percent) is health insurance.

Practice 2

A. Listen to the sentences and circle *er* or *est*. (Example: *Bigger* = *er*; *biggest* = *est*.)

1. er   (est)   **3.** er   est   **5.** er   est

2. er   est   **4.** er   est   **6.** er   est

B. Read the data below and mark the correct answers.

If your taxable income is:	And you are:					Enter your standard deductions.
	Single	Married filing jointly	Married filing separately	Head of a household		**Enter:**
$23,000–$23,050	$3,490	$3,454	$3,977	$3,454		$6,550 if married filing jointly
$23,050–$23,100	$3,504	$3,461	$3,991	$3,461		$5,750 if head of household
						$3,900 if single
						$3,275 if married filing separately

People who earn about $23,000 per year	Single	Married filing jointly	Married filing separately	Head of a household
1. pay the highest taxes if they are	_____	_____	✔	_____
2. pay the least taxes if they are	_____	_____	_____	_____
3. get the largest deductions if they are	_____	_____	_____	_____
4. get the smallest deductions if they are	_____	_____	_____	_____

C. Survey the members of the class about the kinds of payroll deductions they have (on their paychecks). On a separate sheet of paper, list the most common payroll deductions.

3 In 1994, the average American full-time worker earned about $2,000 less than in 1979.

The average worker earned about $2,000 **less** this year **than** in 1979.

The average worker earned about $2,000 **more** in 1979 **than** this year.

Examples

Last week I worked **more** overtime and had a **bigger** paycheck than the month before. But they withheld **more** taxes, **more than** I need to pay. So I'm going to do my W-4 again and claim **more** allowances. Then they will take out **less** tax **than** last week.

Practice 3

A. Listen and read along. Answer by saying who does more than who.

1. Pedro worked 35 hours last week. Eva worked 45 hours.

  Example: Eva worked more hours than Pedro.

2. Marta claims seven allowances on her W-4. Send claims five.

3. Tony supervises eight workers. Salima is foreman over 12 workers.

4. Mark pays $210 a month for health insurance. Lee pays $180 a month for his HMO.

5. Gabrielle spends $120 a week on food for her family, while Luis spends $150 a week.

B. With a partner, do Activity A again. This time, say who does less than who.

C. Work with a partner. Student A: Look at this page. Student B: Look at page 60. The chart below shows what four workers were paid for two weeks of work. Compare data about two employees at a time to complete the chart.

Example:
B: Alice's federal taxes were $10 more than Carlos's.
A: That means Alice's taxes were $69.42, right?
B: No, ten dollars more than Carlos's. $89.42.
A: Oh, yeah. $89.42.

	Alice's Paycheck	Bob's Paycheck	Carlos's Paycheck	Diana's Paycheck
Gross Pay	$ 830		$ 810	$ 660
Federal Taxes		$49.16	$ 79.42	$ 52.60
Overtime	6 hours		16 hours	
Medical Insurance	$ 125.12	$ 65.00		
Net Pay			$ 670.78	$ 582.75

Work with a partner. Student A: Look at page 59. Student B: Look at this page. The chart below shows what four workers were paid for two weeks of work. Compare data about two employees at a time to complete the chart.

Example:
A: Carlos earned $150 more gross pay than Diana.
B: $810 minus $150. So Diana earned $660, right?
A: Right.

	Alice's Paycheck	Bob's Paycheck	Carlos's Paycheck	Diana's Paycheck
Gross Pay	$830	$670	$ 810	
Federal Taxes	$89.42		$79.42	$52.60
Overtime		8 hours		0 hours
Medical Insurance			$85.19	$38.15
Net Pay	$650.22	$458.59		

D. Write five sentences about the employees' salaries and taxes in the chart above. Make calculations and compare two people in each sentence.

Example: *Alice earned $191.63 more net pay than Bob.*

1. _____

2. _____

3. _____

4. _____

5. _____

E. Role-play. Work with a partner. One of you is a supervisor or personnel manager, and the other is a new employee. The new employee does not understand gross pay, net pay, or basic deductions. Why does an employee make more or less take-home pay after certain deductions? Explain to your partner. Change roles.

Putting It to Work

1 Pair Work

Step 1. With a partner, fill out the W-4 form for yourselves. Use the Personal Allowances Worksheet to figure your deductions. Important: Be sure to fill out the form in pencil. Refer to the instructions on page 52.

Personal Allowances Worksheet

A Enter "1" for **yourself** if no one else can claim you as a dependent . . . . **A** _____

B Enter "1" if:
- You are single and have only one job; or
- You are married, have only one job, and your spouse does not work; or
- Your wages from a second job or your spouse's wages (or the total of both) are $1,000 or less.

B _____

C Enter "1" for your **spouse.** But, you may choose to enter -0- if you are married and have either a working spouse or more than one job (this may help you avoid having too little tax withheld) . . . . **C** _____

D Enter number of **dependents** (other than your spouse or yourself) you will claim on your tax return . . . . **D** _____

E Enter "1" if you will file as **head of household** on your tax return (see conditions under **Head of Household** above) . **E** _____

F Enter "1" if you have at least $1,500 of **child or dependent care expenses** for which you plan to claim a credit . . **F** _____

G Add lines A through F and enter total here. **Note:** This amount may be different from the number of exemptions you claim on your return ▶ **G** _____

For accuracy, do all worksheets that apply.
- If you plan to **itemize or claim adjustments to income** and want to reduce your withholding, see the Deductions and Adjustments Worksheet on page 2.
- If you are **single** and have **more than one job** and your combined earnings from all jobs exceed $30,000 OR if you are **married** and have a **working spouse or more than one job,** and the combined earnings from all jobs exceed $50,000, see the Two-Earner/Two-Job Worksheet on page 2 if you want to avoid having too little tax withheld.
- If **neither** of the above situations applies, **stop here** and enter the number from line G on line 5 of Form W-4 below.

- - - - - - - - - - - **Cut here and give the certificate to your employer. Keep the top portion for your records.** - - - - - - - - - - -

Form **W-4** Department of the Treasury Internal Revenue Service	**Employee's Withholding Allowance Certificate** ▶ **For Privacy Act and Paperwork Reduction Act Notice, see reverse.**	OMB No. 1545-0010 **1995**

1 Type or print your first name and middle initial | Last name | **2** Your social security number

Home address (number and street or rural route) | **3** ☐ Single ☐ Married ☐ Married, but withhold at higher Single rate.
Note: If married, but legally separated, or spouse is a nonresident alien, check the Single box.

City or town, state, and ZIP code | **4** If your last name differs from that on your social security card, check here and call 1-800-772-1213 for a new card . . . . . . ▶ ☐

5 Total number of allowances you are claiming (from line G above or from the worksheets on page 2 if they apply) . **5** _____

6 Additional amount, if any, you want withheld from each paycheck . . . . **6** $ _____

7 I claim exemption from withholding for 1995 and I certify that I meet **BOTH** of the following conditions for exemption:
- Last year I had a right to a refund of **ALL** Federal income tax withheld because I had **NO** tax liability; **AND**
- This year I expect a refund of **ALL** Federal income tax withheld because I expect to have **NO** tax liability.
If you meet both conditions, enter "EXEMPT" here . . . . ▶ **7** _____

Under penalties of perjury, I certify that I am entitled to the number of withholding allowances claimed on this certificate or entitled to claim exempt status.

Employee's signature ▶ | **Date** ▶ _____ , 19 _____

8 Employer's name and address (Employer: Complete 8 and 10 only if sending to the IRS) | **9** Office code (optional) | **10** Employer identification number

Cat. No. 10220Q

Step 2. Exchange your forms with another pair of classmates. Check the number of their exemptions. Check the other information on the W-4 forms. Correct them.

Step 3. Look at your classmates' changes to your forms. Discuss them with your partner. Are your forms correct now? Make any final changes necessary.

2 Group/Class Work

Step 1. Work in groups to compare two work situations in the United States with work in your native country. Choose a team leader, a team recorder, and a team reporter.

Step 2. Discuss the questions below about the work situations. Help your team recorder write down your ideas.

1. Who can work? What age limits are there? Are there any work permits or immigration controls?

2. How do people receive their pay? Do they get cash or a paycheck? Or does the employer put money directly into their bank accounts?

3. Are there any taxes? If so, how much do people pay? How do people pay taxes? Do they pay directly from their paychecks? Do tax officials come to their homes? Do they pay everything at the end of the year? Do they go to a special tax office to pay?

Situation 1: Undocumented work. In the United States, many people work without valid legal papers (such as a green card).

Situation 2: Documented work. People in this category are U.S. citizens, or they have a green card or some other legal work authorization.

Situation 3: Work in your native country. _____

Step 3. Your team reporter will report your ideas to the class.

3 Culture Work

Since 1986, it has been the law in the United States that all employers must verify (check) that their workers can legally work in the country. How many in the class remember having to show their Social Security Card, their Resident Alien card, and maybe other identification to their employer?

The name of the 1986 law is the *Immigration Reform and Control Act.* Many companies put a statement in their employee handbook about this law. Here is a statement about the law from one company handbook.

VERIFYING EMPLOYABILITY

The U.S. federal Immigration Reform and Control Act of 1986 required that all employees hired by Robertson and Company, Incorporated, provide documentation that proves they have a legal right to work in the United States.

In order to obey this law, all job offers from Robertson & Co., Inc., are effective only when the company has received the required documentation and a completed INS Form I-9. Only those successful applicants who provide the required documentation and who complete Form I-9 will be permitted to begin work.

Unit 6
COMPANY RULES AND INSTRUCTIONS

Openers

Look at the pictures. Find these things:

name badge   parking decal   company map
W-4 form   time card   flip chart

Jorge has a new job at Fairview Hospital Supplies. Four other new employees are here for their first day on the job. They are in the training room for their orientation with the personnel director. Do you remember your first day at your present or last job?

1 Listen and Think

Listen and choose the correct answers to the questions.

1. Where did Megan and Jorge meet?

2. Has Megan ever been to an orientation?

3. What's Megan's job at the company? What's Jorge's job?

4. Why does Jorge think maintenance sounds like a good job for Megan?

2 Talk to a Partner

Step 1. Practice the conversation with a partner.

> A: Is this your first day on the job?
> B: Yes, it is. I'm a little nervous because
>   I've never worked in a factory.
> A: Don't be nervous. Everyone here works together.
>   Have you ever had to work with machines?
> B: Yes, I have. I like working with machines.
> A: I do, too. I'd rather work in a factory than in a
>   restaurant or a hotel or something.

Step 2. With the same partner, use the information from the job applications and have a conversation like the one above.

APPLICATION FOR EMPLOYMENT *Wilson's Bakery*

Position applied for: <u>baker's assistant</u>
Previous Employment:

<u>Company</u>	<u>Type of Business</u>	<u>Position(s) held</u>
Shoes R Us	shoe store	stocker

APPLICATION FOR EMPLOYMENT *Sleepy Time Hotel*

Position applied for: <u>van driver</u>
Previous Employment:

<u>Company</u>	<u>Type of Business</u>	<u>Position(s) held</u>
Jefferson High School	school	janitor
Super Grocer	grocery store	janitor stocker

APPLICATION FOR EMPLOYMENT *World Telephone*

Position Applied for: <u>telephone repairman</u>
Previous Employment:

<u>Company</u>	<u>Type of Business</u>	<u>Position(s) held</u>
Transitron	electrical circuits	circuit repairer
Mesa manufacturing	factory	machine operator
Wheels, Inc.	bicycle shop	repairer

Step 3. Now use your own information from your present jobs and previous jobs you and your partner have had. Ask each other about your work experience and the kind of work you like doing as in the conversation above.

3 Read and Think

Step 1. Read the text below.

Jorge received a lot of information on his first day at Fairview Hospital Supplies. At the orientation, he received several forms to fill out and some instructions. One of the instruction sheets had a list of rules and regulations that employees must follow while working.

Some of the information in rules and regulations is about:
1. uniforms **2.** work schedules **3.** breaks **4.** employee areas (such as the break room, parking area, smoking area) **5.** general procedures

Step 2. Look at the rules and regulations below. With a partner, find out which kind of information is given in each rule. Try to guess the meaning of any new words.

Fairview Hospital Supplies, Inc.
Rules and Regulations

1. Employees must wear their name badges on company premises.
2. Employees must punch in when arriving and must punch out when leaving each day.
3. Employees may take breaks only at specified break times.
4. Employees must park their cars in the employee parking area only. The parking decal must be clearly visible.

Step 3. Study the vocabulary below and then reread the company rules and regulations.

Vocabulary

premises the building and land occupied or owned by a company or person
punch in/out put a time card in the time clock to have the date and time stamped
orientation a meeting where information is given to people who are new to a situation
specified given a definite time, date, or place
visible can be seen

Step 4. Read the memo preview below.

Reading Memos

Memos are a common form of written communication in companies. Some employees write memos to the entire company or just to groups or individuals in the company. Usually short pieces of information or announcements of some kind, memos often look something like this:

FAIRVIEW HOSPITAL SUPPLIES
Interoffice Memo

September 10, 1997

TO: All employees
FROM: Susana Cortez, Director of Human Resources   *SC*
SUBJECT: Name badges

There is usually a heading at the top with the company name. The **date** is very important since there may be several memos circulating in a company at the same time. The **"TO"** line indicates which employees must read the memo. The **"FROM"** line indicates who wrote the memo. The **"SUBJECT"** of the memo makes it very clear to the reader what the memo is about. The **message** is usually short, no more than one or two paragraphs. Memos are not signed at the bottom like letters, but they are **initialed** at the top by the person who wrote the memo.

Step 5. During his first week at Fairview Hospital Supplies, Jorge saw several memos on the bulletin board near the time clock. Read the memos that Jorge saw on the bulletin board.

FAIRVIEW HOSPITAL SUPPLIES
Interoffice Memo

September 10, 1997

TO: All employees
FROM: Susana Cortez, Director of Human Resources   *SC*
SUBJECT: Name badges

New name badges will be issued to all employees on Friday in the Human Resources office. Be sure to pick up your new name badge before you leave on Friday.

All employees must wear their new name badges beginning on Monday.

FAIRVIEW HOSPITAL SUPPLIES
Interoffice Memo

September 12, 1997

TO: All supervisors
FROM: Bud Sweeney, Chief Engineer *BS*
SUBJECT: New operating manuals

The new operating manuals for the Acme presses have arrived. Please come by my office as soon as possible and pick up your department's copy.

FAIRVIEW HOSPITAL SUPPLIES
Interoffice Memo

September 13, 1997

TO: All new employees
FROM: Len Taylor, Vice-President *LT*
SUBJECT: Meeting

All employees who started working after July 1 must report to a meeting in the cafeteria on Friday, September 15, at 9:00 A.M. to complete some personnel forms. The meeting will last approximately 30 minutes.

Step 6. **With a partner, answer the following questions about the memos you read. Remember that Jorge's first day of work was September 10 and he works in the maintenance department.**

1. Which memo is the oldest? Which one is the newest?
2. Are all of the memos directed to Jorge? Which ones are? Which ones aren't?
3. Which memos require Jorge to do something? What does he have to do? When?
4. Do any memos pertain to the rules and regulations that Jorge received on his first day (see page 65)? Which ones? What additional information did the memos give him about any of the rules and regulations?

Vocabulary

interoffice from one office to another within the same company

initial write the first letter of your first name and last name

bulletin board a large piece of wood or cork hung on a wall to display bulletins (notices, announcements, memos, etc.)

issued given

operating manual a book of instructions for running equipment

from now on beginning now and continuing into the future

interfere get in the way; interrupt

pertain be related to

Practice

Complete the sentences with the correct words.

issued	punch in	bulletin board
orientation	operating manual	visible

1. If your parking decal is not clearly _____*visible*_____ , the company can tow your car.

2. You have to _____ when you begin your shift so your time card is correct.

3. We attended an _____ on the first day to learn the company rules and instructions.

4. I need to look in the _____ to find out how to run this machine.

5. This was my first week of work, so the company has not _____ me a paycheck yet.

6. Please look on the _____ to see if there is an announcement about the meeting.

4 Put It in Writing

Step 1. Think about the place you work now or somewhere you used to work. Write down some of the company rules.

1. _____

2. _____

3. _____

4. _____

Step 2. Now write some rules about things employees must not do at your company.

1. _____

2. _____

3. _____

4. _____

5 Listen and Speak

Step 1. **A new employee is talking about the company policy. Listen to the conversation.**

A: I've never seen so many rules in my life!
Do I have to learn all of these?

B: Yes, you do. But don't worry. You'll be able
to remember them after you're here a while.

A: I've never had a list of rules like this at any other
company. Have you ever seen anything like this?

B: No. I agree. They have a lot of rules here. But the rules
are clear and logical. And I'd rather have a lot of clear
and logical rules than just a few unreasonable rules or
no rules at all. After all, when there aren't any rules or
procedures, you don't know what the company expects.
Then everyone does something different. That can cause conflicts.

Step 2. **Practice the conversation with a partner.**

Step 3. **Continue the conversation. Student A: Ask your partner about the problems at the other company. Student B: Give examples of the problems at your other company.**

Here are some examples of problems at the other company. Add your own.

Employees used to come to work late.
Some people used to take long breaks.

_____

_____

_____

_____

Step 4. **With another pair of classmates talk about the problems that came up at the other company. Ask them about the problems that came up at their company. Were they the same kinds of problems as yours or were they different?**

Step 5. **Have you ever worked at a company where these kinds of problems happened? What did the company do about the problems? Discuss your experiences with your foursome.**

6 Read and Write

Step 1. Read Glenwood Paper Company's list of things to do and not to do.

Glenwood Paper Co.

DO

Arrive on time.
Work only your scheduled shift.
Call at least two hours before
your shift if you are sick.
Wear an appropriate uniform.

DON'T

Smoke in the building.
Park in the customer parking lot.
Work overtime unless it
is approved.
Be on premises unless you are
scheduled to work.

Step 2. Rewrite each item above as a rule or regulation.

1. *All employees must arrive on time.*
2. _____
3. _____
4. _____
5. _____
6. _____
7. _____
8. _____

Step 3. Compare your answers with a partner.

Step 4. On a separate sheet of paper, write some more sentences with *Do* and *Don't*. Give them to your partner.

Step 5. Write a rule for each item on your partner's list.

Form and Function

1 I've never seen so many rules in my life.

| I've, you've, we've, they've he's, she's (it's) | **never seen** | so many rules. |

Examples

Sam's never been late for work. He **has never been** sick either.
I haven't met the new supervisor.
A: **Has** she **ever worked** with us? B: No, she **hasn't**. She **has never worked** in our department.

Practice 1

A. Listen. Circle the correct answer.

1. a. work   (worked)
    b. haven't   have

2. a. has   have
    b. has   have

3. c. talked   talk
    d. hasn't   has

B. Write a question after each statement using the correct forms of the words in parentheses.

Example:

José has never had a full-time job.
(you) (ever) (work) **Have you ever worked** full time?

1. I have never been to Guatemala. (Jerry) (ever) (visit) ____*Has Jerry ever visited*____ Guatemala?

2. No one in this department has ever run this machine. (anyone) (ever) (use) _____

_____ a machine like it?

3. We have never told the company president about this problem.

(our supervisor) (ever) (speak) _____ to him?

4. You have never been to my house. (you) (ever) (go) _____ to
Dora's apartment?

C. On a separate sheet of paper, write down five things you have never done. Then ask your partner if he/she has ever done those things.

2 I'd rather have a lot of clear and logical rules.

I would rather = **I'd rather**

| **Would** | I, you, he, she, it, we, they | **rather** | work or stay home? |
| | I, you, he, she, it, we, they | **would rather** | stay home **than** work. |

Examples

I'd rather work the graveyard shift **than** the day shift because the pay is better.
A: **Would** Rick **rather** work with Marco or Paula?
B: He and Paula don't get along, so I think **he'd rather** work with Marco.

Practice 2

A. Listen. Circle each person's preference.

1. 7:30   (8:00)

2. waitress   cook

3. Los Angeles   San Diego

4. overtime   go home

B. Teresa rated each of the items below on a scale from 1 to 5. A *1* means she doesn't like that activity at all; a *5* means she likes that activity very much. Write four sentences about Teresa's preferences.

Example:

Teresa would rather wash dishes than mow the lawn.

Activity	Teresa's Rating
wash dishes	2
mow the lawn	1
cook	5
vacuum	3
pay bills	4

C. Now write down five of your household chores and rate them on a scale from 1 to 5. Then tell your partner about your preferences.

Putting It to Work

1 Pair Work

Step 1. Listen to the personnel director speaking at an orientation session. With a partner, fill in the missing information in the company rules below.

1. _____ for your scheduled shift.

2. When you arrive at work, _____ at the time clock.

3. You need to _____ at all times while you are working.

4. _____ in the north parking lot. You may park in the south lot or the east lot.

5. You must call your department supervisor _____ your scheduled shift if you are sick.

6. _____ , you must leave the company premises.

7. All overtime work _____ by your supervisor.

8. _____ near the entrance for announcements about meetings and policy changes.

Step 2. Does your employer have rules like these? How did you learn the rules? Tell your partner some of the rules at your job and how you learned them.

2 Pair Work

Step 1. Role-play.

Student A: It's your first day at a new job. You have lots of questions about the company, the procedures, and where things are.

Student B: You are a long-time employee at this company and you know all the rules and procedures. You want to help the new employee.

Step 2. Now that you know some of the rules, make yourself a list so you can remember them.

Step 3. Change roles.

3 Group/Class Work

Step 1. In a group, imagine you are managers of a new company that is going to open soon. Work together to develop a brief description of your company that includes:

1. the type of company
2. the number of employees
3. the location
4. the name of the company

Step 2. Plan an orientation for your new employees. Decide what information you will give them and how you will give them the information. Make any forms or lists you want to give to them at the orientation.

Step 3. Choose someone (or more than one person) from your group to conduct the orientation. Choose students from the other groups to play your new employees.

Step 4. Conduct your orientation in front of the class. Be sure to let the new employees ask questions.

4 Culture Work

Raul was working at ABC Company for one week, and he arrived ten minutes late for work one morning. His supervisor talked to him about it later that morning.

A: Raul, I wanted to talk to you because you were late this morning.

B: Yes, I'm sorry about that.

A: You know, when you're late, your team has to do your work for you until you get here. That's not fair to them. I'm going to dock you ten minutes' pay.

B: OK. I'm sorry. It won't happen again.

Discuss the questions below with the class.

How might this conversation be different at a company in your native country?
What do you think will happen if Raul is late again next week?
What do you think will happen if Raul breaks another company rule?
What would happen to Raul at a company in your native country?

Unit 7
TEAMWORK

Openers

Look at the picture and identify the following things and people:

conference table   flip chart   manager   team members

Where is Jorge? What is his supervisor talking about? What kinds of changes are taking place at the company? Have you ever been in a situation like this?

1 Listen and Think

Listen and choose the best answers to the questions.

1. Why is the company making changes?

   a. Production is down.

   b. The employees have demanded change.

   c. Salaries are too high.

2. What do the changes involve?

   a. More control over the employees.

   b. A cut in benefits.

   c. A new way of working.

2 Talk to a Partner

Step 1. **Practice the conversation with a partner.**

A: I'm worried about the situation in this company.
B: Oh, really? Why?
A: Ted Turan, my supervisor, is causing problems for people.
B: Ted Turan? What's he doing?
A: Well, last week, he said to us, "Production is down.
   People aren't working hard enough." But he took the
   best people off the job three months ago! And since then,
   he's given a lot of responsibility to this new person, Ralph Wall.
   Ralph's OK, I guess, but he's still learning about the company.
B: But what about our new team structure? We're all going to
   work in teams, aren't we?
A: That hasn't started yet.
B: Maybe you should talk to the Human Resources Manager.

Step 2. **With your partner, identify the main problem in this situation. Then think about the cause or causes of that problem.**

Step 3. **With your partner, discuss this question: What other information do you need to understand the situation at this company?**

Step 4. **Discuss some possible solutions to the problems of the company. List three or four ideas.**

Step 5. **Discuss the limitations on your solutions. Remember: You don't have all of the information about the company.**

3 Read and Think

Step 1. **Work with a partner. What do you know about teamwork? What ideas and words do you know for this topic? On a separate sheet of paper, make a word map like the one below. Add all the words you can think of.**

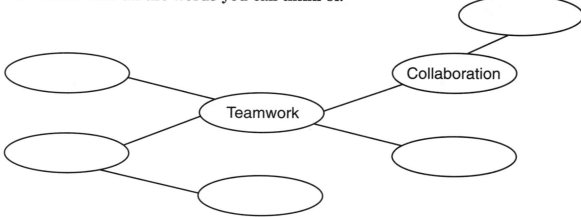

Step 2. Read the title of the document below. What do you think this document says?

Step 3. Read the beginning of the table of contents of the document.

Fairview Hospital Supplies, Inc.
Teamwork for Improved Productivity

Contents

1. Group Collaboration

2. Good Use of Employees' Talents and Skills

3. Shared Leadership

Step 4. Read the first paragraph of the first chapter of the document. Try to guess the meaning of any unfamiliar vocabulary from the context.

When a team works together to make a decision, the decision-making process can take longer. However, the results can take more possibilities into account and can be more creative. When people work on a team, everyone feels responsible for decisions and will be committed to them. If the team receives complete and clear information and if the team members respect each other, workable decisions will result, and the whole organization can benefit.

Step 5. Look at the vocabulary below and then reread the contents and the first paragraph of the text.

Vocabulary

productivity how much a company produces in a specific period of time
collaboration working together as a group
creative having the ability to create, or make, something
be committed to be in strong agreement to do something

Step 6. Use a dictionary to look up any other unfamiliar words and read the texts again.

Step 7. Look back at the table of contents of the document on page 77 and then read the paragraph below. The paragraph is from the second chapter of the teamwork document. Try to guess the meaning of any unfamiliar vocabulary from the context.

Team leaders and team members must recognize and understand the talents and skills of all the members. Each team member's task should be the right task for that person. When a company or a team does not recognize an employee's skills and talents in a specific area, the results can be very negative for the team as a whole. Negative feelings and resentment can develop over time, and such a situation can hurt company productivity.

Step 8. Look up any unfamiliar words in a dictionary and reread the text.

4 Put It in Writing

Step 1. What do you think the qualities of a good team leader are? What are the qualities of a good team player? Write at least three sentences for each. You may use the words below or any others you know.

Adjectives		Noun phrases	Verbs
cooperative	open	a good listener	respect
respectful	understanding	a good observer	share information

Example:

A good team leader should be a good listener. He or she should respect the other team members.

Team Leader

1. _____

2. _____

3. _____

Team Player

1. _____

2. _____

3. _____

Step 2. Now choose either your sentences about team leaders or your sentences about team players. Write one more sentence as a general introduction to the subject.

Example: _A good team leader has many important qualities._

Step 3. Copy your general introductory sentence onto a separate sheet of paper. Then copy your other sentences onto your paper and form a paragraph.

Step 4. With another classmate, exchange your papers. Correct your classmate's sentences and then look at the corrections to your paragraph.

5 Listen and Speak

Step 1. Listen to the conversation.

A: Yussif, you've been here for three months now, haven't you?

B: Yes, since July.

A: Since July? Well, I'd just like to know your impressions of the company.

B: I like it. I have no complaints.

A: Well, that's good. But I'd like to talk about possible improvements at our company. Maybe we could do some things better.

B: I don't know. Everything's fine with me.

A: You know, it's OK to say, "Look, there's something wrong here," when you see something wrong. Tell me this: What would you really like to do at this company?

B: Well, I'd like to have a position of more responsibility. Not right away, of course, but in the future.

A: Of course. That's natural. Anything else?

B: I'd like to learn more about the production system here. I'd like to receive some training on the X-400 machine.

Step 2. Practice the conversation with a partner.

Step 3. Role-play a similar situation between a team leader and a team member (or team player). Tell your team leader what you would like to do in the company. With your partner, change roles between the team leader and the team member.

6 Read and Write

Step 1. Read the action plan for Fairview Hospital Supplies.

6-1-97

Action Plan

Goal: Improvement of teamwork and management-employee relations

Steps: Teams, and the company as a whole, can maximize productivity through some of the following principles:

1. Take time to explore your employees' goals for improvement and personal development on the job.

2. Do not challenge employees with statements like "You said Tuesday. So it has to be Tuesday."

3. If there are problems with production, delivery, or shipping schedules, try to hold a brief meeting to discuss the problems. Ask for suggestions from the team members.

4. Do not simply force your decisions on the team. Try to establish a collaborative decision-making atmosphere.

5. Employees should enjoy coming to work. Try to create an enjoyable work environment for the members of your team.

Step 2. On a separate sheet of paper, answer the questions.

1. Should team members' goals and interests be important to managers?

2. What should managers do when there are problems with schedules?

3. Would a collaborative work environment increase productivity? If yes, why?

4. What do you think managers can do to create an enjoyable work environment?

Step 3. With a partner, compare your answers.

Form and Function

1 Last week he said, "Production is down. People aren't working hard enough."

> Joe: "Production is down. People aren't working hard enough."
>
> **Joe said, "Production is down. People aren't working hard enough."**

Examples

I was talking to my supervisor about the problem, and **she said, "Listen. Don't worry about it. Everything will be OK."**
We were talking about the new policy when **our team leader** walked in and **said, "Forget about that policy. Management has just cancelled it."**

Practice 1

A. Listen and circle " " or —.

1. (" ")　　　　—　　　　3. " "　　　—　　　5. " "　　　　—
2. " "　　　　　—　　　　4. " "　　　—　　　6. " "　　　　—

B. Rewrite the sentences below. Think of the specific time for each sentence.

1. Mary: "We need to meet more often. We have a number of serious work problems." (yesterday)

   Yesterday Mary said, "We need to meet more often. We have a number of serious work problems."

2. Mr. Cranston: "Our company values highly skilled employees." (tomorrow in a speech)

   _____

3. Chan: "Give me five minutes and I'll fix it." (always, when someone has a computer problem)

   _____

4. Roberta: "I'm going to discuss this problem with the rest of the team." (last week)

   _____

C. Can you think of something someone said about your work? Tell a partner. Give the quote word-for-word.

2 A: You've been here for three months now, haven't you?
B: Yes, since July.

I, you, we, they	**have been**	here	**for three months** now.
he, she, it	**has been**		

For (length of time)	**Since** (a starting point)
three months	last week
a year	1984
a long time	I was born
my whole life	yesterday

Examples

A: How long have you been at this company? B: Oh, **for about four years.**
A: We**'ve** lived in this area **for about two years** now. B: **Since 1995?** A: Yes, that's right. **Since 1995.**
The company **has been** in business **since the Gulf War. Since 1991.**
A: You**'ve lived** in this area **for a long time, haven't you?** B: Yes, we**'ve been** here **since 1986.**

Practice 2

A. Listen and circle the words you hear.

1. for (since)   3. for   since   5. for   since

2. for   since   4. for   since   6. for   since

B. Complete each sentence with the correct choice, *for* or *since*.

1. I don't really know the company rules because I've only been here _____*since*_____ July.

2. A: How long have you worked at this company? B: Oh, _____ about five years.

3. We've had problems with this equipment _____ Tuesday.

4. They've lived in this area _____ a very long time.

5. A: I didn't see you come in. How long have you been here? B: Oh, _____ about an hour.

6. I haven't seen Antonia _____ the meeting this morning.

7. A: Has he finished the job yet? B: No, he hasn't done anything _____ 9:00 this morning.

8. Where have you been _____ the last hour?

9. I haven't had time to read a book _____ July.

10. They haven't had a chance to sit down _____ eight hours.

C. Complete the sentences in the paragraph below with *has, have, hasn't, haven't, for,* or *since*.

Plant manager Ted Turan _____*has*_____ been in his office _____ the last two hours,

and his door is closed. Ted and his entire department _____ had a lot of work _____

January, when management increased production goals for the company. Now they have a serious

problem: they (not) _____ been able to meet the most recent production quota. Ted has

to explain this to his boss, so Ted's nervous. _____ this morning, Ted _____

yelled at three of his employees, and two of them _____ quit. Things (not) _____
gone well for Ted this week, and now they probably won't get any better soon.

D. Interview three classmates and ask questions to complete the chart. Write each person's name in the chart. Use *for* and *since*. Follow the example.

Example:
A: How long have you lived in the U.S.?
B: For two years.
A: Oh. Since June 1995?
B: That's right.

Name	Lived in the U.S. for . . .	Since (confirm your guess)	Studied English (for)	Since (confirm your guess)

Putting It to Work

1 Pair Work

Step 1. Listen to the conversation about the situation at Fairview Hospital Supplies and add to the meeting notes below.

Teamwork training: We've scheduled it. People are enthusiastic.

Production quotas: Increase right now creates possible problems.

Suppliers: Suppliers say they're ready.

Question: How can we help team members give suggestions and ideas for the company?

Other:

Step 2. With a partner, look at your notes. What is a positive force in this situation? What is negative? Remember: The company plans to increase teamwork. Talk about the situation and note the positive and negative forces below.

+ Positive force (Favoring quality teamwork)   − Negative force (Preventing quality teamwork)

People are enthusiastic about it.	Some people aren't ready.

Step 3. With your partner, imagine that you work at Fairview Hospital Supplies. Choose one thing to improve in the work situation. With your partner, set a goal for improvement. Save your work.

2 Group/Class Work

Step 1. With your partner from the last activity, form a group of four with another pair of students. Choose a team leader, a team recorder, and a team reporter. Compare your notes on the positive and negative forces at Fairview Hospital Supplies. Discuss the differences you find. Compare your improvement goals.

Step 2. Pool all of your other notes on the work situation at the company. Compare your work and create a group set of notes.

Step 3. Choose an improvement goal from among your entire set of goals.

Step 4. Think of several possible ways to reach your goal. Write your ideas down, along with the consequences and limitations of each idea.

Example:

Goal: Improve quality of finished products.

Idea: Have a group discussion of this goal with the employees, management, and the new team leaders.

Limitations: Management is in a position of power, and the employees are not.

Consequences: The discussion could have good results, but certain managers might intimidate the employees and prevent any real team building.

Step 5. Choose the best idea. Create an action plan for the situation.

Action Plan

Improvement goal:_____

_____

Steps: 1. _____

         _____

        2. _____

         _____

        3. _____

         _____

Step 6. Your group reporter will tell the class about your improvement goal and your plan. Discuss your ideas with the rest of the class and evaluate the plans of the other groups.

3 Culture Work

With the class, look at the pictures below and discuss the questions.

Does leadership belong to only one person?
Should one person always be a leader, or can anyone be a leader?
What is the correct relationship between a leader and the members of a team?
Should employees offer criticism, or should they keep it to themselves?
Is there good criticism, as well as bad criticism?

"Well, I think we've come to a decision."

"I told you to get the tools! What's wrong with you?"

"Shh! There's the boss. Let's discuss this problem later."

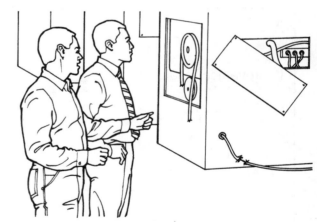

"It happened an hour ago. We'll need to call someone in for this."

Unit 8
CONFLICTS AT WORK

Openers

Look at the pictures and identify the following:

boxes   a crate   a fork lift   parts

Where is Jorge? Why is he upset? What do you think is happening? Have you ever been in a situation like this?

1 Listen and Think

Listen and choose the best answer for each question below.

1. What happened between Jorge and Pierre?
   a. Pierre criticized Jorge, and Jorge became upset.
   b. Jorge insulted Pierre, and they started to fight.
   c. Pierre refused to talk to Jorge, and Jorge became angry.

2. Why did this situation start between Jorge and Pierre?
   a. Jorge couldn't finish his job on time.
   b. Pierre was in a bad mood.
   c. Both Jorge and Pierre are working too hard, and they are becoming impatient.

2 Talk to a Partner

Step 1. Chan and Harvey are discussing the lastest developments at work. Practice the conversation with a partner.

Chan: You're on the accident-prevention team, aren't you?
Harvey: What accident-prevention team?
Chan: You haven't heard?
Harvey: No, what is it?
Chan: Ted's formed a group to examine the number of accidents at the plant and find ways to avoid them.
Harvey: He hasn't told me about it. I wonder why not.
Chan: Well, he just started it yesterday. Maybe he hasn't had time to tell everyone yet.
Harvey: Anyway, your people on the factory floor ought to be a bit more careful. Then we wouldn't have these problems.
Chan: Boy, you're in a lousy mood today. It's not their fault, you know. We have a number of basic safety problems.
Harvey: Listen, I'm sorry. I've had a rough day.

Step 2. With a partner, discuss these questions: Does Harvey's attitude represent a problem for the team? Why? What should Harvey do differently?

Step 3. With your partner, create a follow-up to the conversation. Role-play the parts of Chan and Harvey. Think of a way to avoid tension after this situation. How would you do that?

3 Read and Think

Step 1. Read the first four lines of the memo below. What do you think this document says?

Step 2. Read the text of the memo.

5-5-97

To: All employees
From: Jim Searle   *JS*
Re: Training in team building/conflict resolution

Please read the attached booklet on team building and conflict resolution. This will supplement our training, which begins next Friday. Everyone should take this opportunity to improve their conflict-resolution skills.

Step 3. With a partner, discuss this question: What do you think this memo means for the company?

Step 4. Read the title of the document below. The document is part of a page from the company manual on teamwork. What do you think the document says?

Step 5. Read the text of the document. Try to guess the meaning of any unfamiliar words from the context.

Team Building and Conflict Resolution

Conflict occurs when there are specific problems within an organization. Managers and team leaders must work with their team members to resolve such problems for the good of the team. To do this, everyone must work together and cooperate.

Traditionally, managers used their authority to force employees to accept decisions. We now know that this style of management can have a negative effect on productivity. We all work most efficiently and productively when we think that our ideas are important to the company. When everyone—including the boss—makes an effort to listen, employees understand that they have an important role within the organization.

Consensus, or agreement upon goals, is important for successful teamwork and conflict resolution. Team members must share the same goals for the team. Nevertheless, team members must accept everyone's individuality. They must identify their own differences and learn to work with other people and value their diversity. Differences among people are advantages, not disadvantages, because we all have different skills and abilities.

When each team member can see that the others are valuable members of the company, successful team building can occur. Conflicts may still arise, but the team structure will help everyone to resolve them successfully.

Step 6. Look up any unfamiliar words in the dictionary. Then read the text of the document again.

Step 7. With the class, discuss this question: What does this document mean for Fairview Hospital Supplies?

Practice

Complete the sentences with the words below.

authority	consensus	diversity
efficiently	cooperate	team building

1. Usually, _____*team building*_____ can best occur when everyone is a valued and respected member of the team.

2. In the past, managers made all of the decisions and used their _____ to make people accept those decisions.

3. In a team people work together. If they want to work together well, they need to have

   a _____ about their goals.

4. Everyone is different from everyone else, and team members have to respect

   others' _____.

5. When there is agreement on goals, people can _____.

6. People work _____ when they think their ideas are important to the company.

4 Put It in Writing

Step 1. **With a partner, talk about the kinds of conflicts you have experienced with co-workers. Together, list incidents and types of situations.**

Example: Incident—*A co-worker and I had an argument about paperwork. He wanted to do it one way, and I wanted to do it another way.* Type of situation—*Disagreement about work.*

Incident _____

_____

_____

Type of Situation _____

_____

_____

Step 2. Work individually. When do conflicts occur with people on the job? Write three sentences on this subject. Start one of your sentences with "Conflicts occur when . . ."

1. _____

2. _____

3. _____

Step 3. On a separate sheet of paper, combine your sentences to form a paragraph.

Step 4. Show your paragraph to your partner. Correct your partner's paragraph and then look at your partner's corrections to your paragraph. Discuss any disagreements.

5 Listen and Speak

Step 1. Listen to the conversation.

A: There's been a lot of conflict here lately, and we
need to do something about it.
B: Well, here's my suggestion: management ought
to bring more employees into the decision-making process.
More people need to—
A: We've already set up teams and teamwork. That's
a big enough step for now.
B: Maybe we should go further. Safety at the plant is
a big issue right now, and we should ask everyone for
their suggestions, get people together in—
A: No, look, we reached a decision on that last week.
And it's final. We're not going to do it.
B: Well, then, what do you suggest?
A: We might have to have stricter policies around here.
B: And that's going to decrease tension?
A: The tension will stop when people realize their jobs
are on the line.

Step 2. Practice the conversation with a partner.

Step 3. With your partner, think about the power relationship between the two speakers. Which person is more important in the company? Do you think one works under the other? Why or why not?

Step 4. With your partner, discuss this question: What is wrong with A's ideas?

6 Read and Write

Step 1. Read the memo on conflicts and behavior.

To: All employees
From: Jim Searle *JS*
Re: Conflicts and unacceptable behavior

Unacceptable behavior:
Fairview Hospital Supplies provides employees with a professional work environment free from physical, psychological, or verbal harrassment. The company does not allow the following types of behavior:

- Insults
- Fighting
- Insulting jokes about women or men

- Jokes about people from different countries or different racial or ethnic groups
- Unwanted physical contact
- Display of pornography or other similar pictures of women or men

Conflicts:
   If you cannot resolve a conflict through your supervisor, please see Pamela Alvarez, our Assistant Human Resources Manager. She will take care of any conflict resolution problems between employees.
   The list above is not complete. If you have any questions, please see me or Pamela Alvarez.

Step 2. Answer the questions.

1. Can employees put up pictures of men or women in their work areas? _No, they can't._ ____

   _____

2. What kinds of jokes are unacceptable at Fairview Hospital Supplies? _____

   _____

3. What kinds of pictures are unacceptable at Fairview Hospital Supplies? _____

   _____

4. Should employees go to their supervisors if there is a conflict with another employee? _____

   _____

5. What else can employees do when there is a conflict with another employee? _____

   _____

Step 3. With a partner, compare your answers.

Form and Function

1 I'm sorry. I've had a rough day.

Simple Apologies	Strong Apologies	Explanations/Excuses
I'm sorry.	I'm *really* sorry.	I've had a rough day.
I apologize.	I'm *very* sorry.	It was a mistake/an accident.
	I'm *so* sorry.	I didn't mean it.
	Please forgive me.	It wasn't intentional.

Examples

I'm *so* sorry. What a terrible mistake! I just forgot! **I'm sorry.**
I'm *really* sorry. I didn't mean that. **I sincerely apologize.**
A: You interrupted me! B: **Oh, I'm sorry.**
A: That's offensive! That's a terrible thing to say! B: **I'm *really* sorry!** I didn't mean it like that.
A: You called me a liar! B: I'm really sorry. Please forgive me. I didn't mean it. I was just upset.

Practice 1

A. Listen to each apology and circle Simple or Strong.

1. (simple)   strong   **3.** simple   strong   **5.** simple   strong

2. simple   strong   **4.** simple   strong   **6.** simple   strong

B. Match the sentences on the left with appropriate apologies on the right.

You dropped that on my toe!   I'm sorry.

You spilled coffee on my shirt!   I'm very sorry.

This part is in the wrong place.   I'm so sorry!

C. Work with a partner. Role-play one of the following situations:

Situation 1: You pass someone in a hall and accidentally bump him/her. The other person is carrying coffee, and that person spills the coffee on the floor. **Student A:** Tell your partner he/she bumped into you. **Student B:** Apologize. Change roles.

Situation 2: You arrive late to work and immediately see your supervisor. **Student A:** Tell your partner he/she is late. **Student B:** Apologize. Change roles.

2 Management ought to bring more employees into the decision-making process.

| Management | **ought to** (should) | bring more employees into the decision-making process. |
| I, you, he, she, it, we, they | | |

Usage note: Question forms of *ought to* are not common in American English. Instead, people say, "Do you think (I, you, he, she, we, they) ought to . . . ?"

Examples

We **ought to** get together and talk about these new changes at the company.
A: **Do you really think** we **ought to?** B: Yes, I think we **ought to.**
A: This job demands so much work! I'm under heavy stress! B: You **ought to** relax. Maybe you **ought to** take a few days off.

Practice 2

A. Listen and circle True or False.

1. Masha should go to the dentist.	T	F
2. Jeff should talk to a doctor.	T	F
3. Abdallah should talk to the Human Resources Manager.	T	F
4. Ted should hold more meetings with his team.	T	F

B. Look at the pictures below. What do you think these people ought to do? On a separate sheet of paper, write a sentence for each picture.

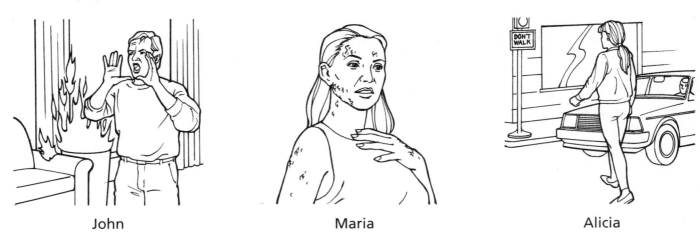

John   Maria   Alicia

C. Tell a partner what you think about these people.

3 A: He hasn't told me about it. I wonder why not.
B: He just started it yesterday. Maybe he hasn't had time to tell everyone yet.

He **started** it	yesterday.	He	**hasn't had**	time to tell everyone	**yet.**
	last week.				
	last month.	I	**have had**	a rough day (*today*).	
	last year.				
	two days ago.				

Examples

A: **Have** you **finished** that job? B: Yes, I **finished** it yesterday.
A: **How long have** you **been** at this company? B: Since **I came** to Los Angeles **five years ago.**

Practice 3

A. Listen and circle the words you hear.

1. worked ⟨has worked⟩

2. finished   has finished

3. stopped   have stopped

4. didn't punch out   hasn't punched out

5. heard   have heard

6. didn't take   haven't taken

B. Work with a partner. Student A: Look at this page. Student B: Look at page 96. Ask your partner questions and complete the chart.

Key: ✔ = yes; ✗ = no.

Example:
B: Has Tom finished the report?
A: Yes, he has.
B: When did he do it?
A: Yesterday.

Person	Activity	Time
Tom	Finish the report ✔	Yesterday
Rachel	Repair the radio	
Allison	Clean up her work area ✗	—
Maria	Fill out her time card	
Omar	Wash the windows ✔	Two hours ago
Fatima	Make the photocopies	

Work with a partner. Student B: Look at this page. Student A: Look at page 95. Ask your partner questions and complete the chart.

Key: ✔ = yes; ✘ = no.

Example:

A: Has Rachel repaired the radio?
B: Yes, she has.
A: When did she do it?
B: On Wednesday.

Person	Activity	Time
Tom	Finish the report	
Rachel	Repair the radio ✔	On Wednesday
Allison	Clean up her work area	
Maria	Fill out her time card ✔	Twenty minutes ago
Omar	Wash the windows	
Fatima	Make the photocopies ✘	—

C. Now write one sentence about each person in the chart. If the person has done the activity, give the time. Use the correct tense, the present perfect or the simple past.

1. Tom _____

2. Rachel _____

3. Allison _____

4. Maria _____

5. Omar _____

6. Fatima _____

Putting It to Work

1 Pair Work

Step 1. Listen to the conversation about recent conflicts at Fairview Hospital Supplies. What changes have occurred? Complete the list.

Meeting with Arthur, Teresa, and Shelly, 4–7–97

Recent changes:
New schedules   More overtime for the second shift

Step 2. With a partner, look at your notes. What is a positive force in this company? What is negative? Brainstorm a list of positive and negative forces. Remember: The company's goal is to improve communication.

+ Positive force (Favoring communication)

People have a lot of ideas and want to share them.

− Negative force (Preventing communication)

People have more work and less time to communicate.

Step 3. With your partner, review your notes from above and from other units. Think of some ways to improve communication on the job. Write your ideas on a separate sheet of paper and save them.

2 Group/Class Work

Step 1. With your partner from the last activity, form a group of four with another pair of students. Choose a team leader, a team recorder, and a team reporter. Pool all of your notes and compare your ideas for improvement of communication.

Step 2. Discuss the consequences and limitations of each idea.

Step 3. Choose the best idea and create an action plan.

Action Plan

Improvement goal: _To improve communication at Fairview Hospital Supplies,_

1. between employees and 2. between employees and managers

Steps: 1. _____

_____

2. _____

_____

3. _____

_____

Step 4. Your group reporter will tell the class about your improvement goal and your plan. Discuss your ideas with the rest of the class and evaluate the plans of the other groups.

3 Culture Work

People have different responses to conflict with co-workers.

In a conflict, some people argue with their co-workers.
Some people run away from conflicts.
Some people feel terrible and can't work after a conflict.
Some people want to fight.
What do you do when you have a conflict with someone on the job?

Discuss this question with the class.

Openers

Look at the pictures and identify the following:

conference table   chart   production line   profits

PROFITS ↓

Production

Revenues
Costs
FTEs

Where are the employees? What is the boss discussing? Have you ever been in a situation like this? What was it like?

1 Listen and Think

Listen and circle True or False.

1. Company profits were higher six months ago.   (T)   F

2. Fairfield Hospital Supplies is improving financially.   T   F

3. Recent months have shown an increase in company profits.   T   F

4. Company profits are continuing to decrease.   T   F

5. Profits might improve if more workers were employed.   T   F

2 Talk to a Partner

Step 1. **Practice the conversation with a partner.**

A: We're here to talk about our production figures. Production has fallen behind in the past two months.
B: No, it hasn't. We've shipped the same quantity this quarter as last quarter.
A: But now we need to produce more. True—we've done about twelve thousand units this quarter, and we did about the same number before. But our orders are higher now.
B: Well, what can we do about it? People are producing as much as they can.
A: We're going to have to monitor our production levels very carefully. And we can ask all of the different teams for suggestions on production increases.

	1st quarter	2nd quarter
Syringes	12,000 units	12,000 units
Gloves	40,500 units	40,000 units
Protective Masks	38,300 units	41,800 units

Step 2. **Look at the chart above. Role-play a similar conversation in a meeting. Compare this quarter's production level with last quarter's production level.**

3 Read and Think

Step 1. **Look at the heading for the chart below. Then look at the gray areas.**

Step 2. **With a partner, read the whole chart. Find the following information:**

Approximate number of orders for January to March
Approximate number of units produced for the same quarter

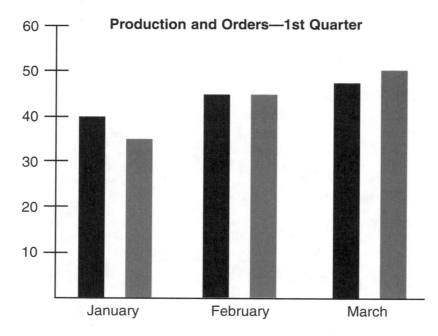

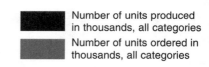
Number of units produced in thousands, all categories
Number of units ordered in thousands, all categories

Step 3. Calculate the difference in the figures for production and orders from one month to the next and tell the class your results.

4 Put It in Writing

Step 1. Work with a partner. Discuss this question: How much classwork have you done over the last two months? Brainstorm a list of tasks. Put your classwork into categories: Homework, Writing in Class, and Out-of-Class Activities.

Step 2. Work individually. On a separate sheet of paper, begin a memo about classwork to your teacher. Fill in the date and the first three lines for a memo.

      Example: January 10

                  To:
                  From:
                  Subject:

Step 3. Put the headings Homework, Writing in Class, and Out-of-Class Activities on your memo. Leave space for several sentences after each heading.

      Homework:

      Writing in Class:

Step 4. Write a sentence for each item on your list.

Step 5. Which class activities or assignments have you been unable to do? Why? Make a second list and include your reasons.

Step 6. List the assignments you haven't done after the heading Unfinished Work (or Work Not Done). List the assignments and give a reason for each item.

Step 7. With your partner, compare your work.

5 Listen and Speak

Step 1. Listen to the conversation.

A: How can we increase our production levels?

B: Look, this week we've produced 5,000 catheters and 23,000 syringes. Today alone, we've already done about three thousand units.

A: Yes, but how are we going to increase that?

B: We can't do anything without more employees. If we have more people, then we can increase production.

C: I'm sure we can increase production without extra employees. We just have to change our production line. I think it's just too far from the production line to the warehouse.

A: No, it's not. A forklift can get anything from the warehouse to the production line in two minutes. We need new equipment. Our presses are too old. The latest models are much faster.

C: We don't have money for new equipment. We have to change our production line.

B: We could hire more people for the night shift. Then we could definitely increase our output.

Step 2. In a group of three, practice the conversation. Each person takes one role.

Step 3. Choose a team leader, a team reporter, and a team recorder. Role-play a similar meeting and take a position for or against the positions in the conversation.

Step 4. Your team reporter will report your ideas for and against to the class.

6 Read and Write

Step 1. Read the production schedule.

> ### South Section Production Schedule: May
>
> **May 1–5:** 15,000 catheters; 5,000 paper gowns; 8,000 disposable syringes
> **May 8–12:** 15,500 catheters; 6,000 paper gowns; 8,000 disposable syringes
> **May 15–19:** 15,700 catheters; 7,000 paper gowns; 8,400 disposable syringes

Step 2. On a separate sheet of paper, write answers to the questions.

1. How many units do the employees have to produce from May 1 to May 5?

2. How many units do they have to produce from May 8 to May 12?

3. How many units do they have to produce for the entire month of May?

4. What is the difference between the first week of May and the second week of May?

5. Why do you think there is a difference?

Step 3. With a partner, compare your answers.

Form and Function

1 People are producing as much as they can.

People are	producing	**as much**	—	**as** they can.
People are**n't**		**as many**	—	
		as much paper	**as many** syringes	

Examples

We're doing **as much as** we can. You're **not** doing **as much as** you can—you could do more.
We're producing **as many boxes as** we can. We can't produce any more.

Practice 1

A. Listen and circle the words you hear.

1. as much . . . as   (as many . . . as)   **3.** as much . . . as   as many . . . as

2. as much as . . .   as many . . . as   **4.** as much . . . as   as many. . . as

B. Look at the simple bar charts. Are people producing as much as they can? On a separate sheet of paper, write a sentence for each chart.

1. AVC, Inc.: Paper
Capacity ▰▰▰
Production ▰▰▰

2. OmniCo.: Glue
Capacity ▰▰▰
Production ▰▰

3. Glazer & Co.: Containers
Capacity ▰▰
Production ▰▰▰

C. Tell a partner about the companies above.

2 Today alone, we've produced about 3,000 units.

Aston Paper Co.			
	Today	This Week	Last Week
Premium-grade paper:	20 tons	100 tons	97
Low-grade paper:	30 tons	140 tons	136

Examples

We**'ve produced** 20 tons of premium-grade paper today. We**'ve produced** 100 tons of premium-grade paper this week. Last week, we **produced** 97 tons.

I**'ve run** 5 miles already. We**'ve finished** five batches so far. The company **has made** a lot of money this year. Production **has increased** 29 percent this year.

Practice 2

A. Listen and circle the phrases you hear.

1. a. have produced 4,000 this week 2. a. have done 300 batches today 3. a. have made 400 boxes today

   b. produced 4,000 last week   b. did 300 batches yesterday   b. made 400 boxes yesterday

B. Look at the chart on the bottom of page 103. On a separate sheet of paper, write sentences for each level of production of the low-grade paper.

Example: (For premium-grade paper) We've produced 20 tons of premium-grade paper today.

C. How much homework have you done this week? this month? How much have you read? What about last month? Tell a partner.

3 I'm sure we can increase production without extra employees.

I'm, you're, we're, they're he's, she's		**sure**	(that)	we **can** increase production.
Are	you	**sure**	(that)	we **can** increase production?

Examples

I'm sure we **can** find the problem. We can **definitely** find the problem. **I'm sure** of it.
I'm sure that everything **will work** out. **I'm certain** we can come to an agreement.
Are you **certain** that the delivery **is** for today? Yes, **I'm positive**.
I'm positive that we **received** those supplies last Tuesday.

Practice 3

A. Listen and circle *one* if you hear one clause and *two* if you hear two clauses.

1. one   two   **3.** one   two   **5.** one   two   **7.** one   two

2. one   two   **4.** one   two   **6.** one   two   **8.** one   two

B. Three companies have made the decisions below. With a partner, talk about each company separately. Can the company increase production? Are you sure or not? Use the expressions above.

Company 1. Hire more people.
Company 2. Hire more people and buy better machinery.
Company 3. Tell the employees to work faster.

C. Write a sentence about each company. Use the expressions in the examples above.

4 If we hire more people, we can increase production.

| If we hire | more people, | we **can increase** | production. |
| **We can increase** | production | **if** we **hire** | more people. |

Examples

If we **change** our production line, we **can increase** production. **If** we **have** enough money, we **can buy** some really good equipment. **If** the company **doesn't have** enough money, it **can't buy** new equipment. **If** you **use** a forklift, you **can take** supplies from the warehouse to the production line in two minutes. **If** the computers **aren't working**, we **can't do** any work.

Practice 4

A. Listen and circle "if , —" when the if clause comes first. Circle "— if" when it comes second.

1. ⟨if , —⟩   — if   2. if , —   — if   3. if , —   — if

B. Match the phrases on the left with the phrases on the right. A number of sentences are possible. Copy your sentences onto a separate sheet of paper. Then, with a partner, compare your work and correct it.

if the company hires temporary workers
if the company buys better equipment
if the employees don't work hard enough
if the machines aren't working today
if the employees work well together

nobody can work
the company can't increase production
the company can increase production
the company can have a collaborative team
   enviroment

C. Work with a partner. Student A: Look at this page only. Student B: Look at page 106. Talk about the problems below. Choose a solution from the chart. Complete the chart with your partner's ideas. Use expressions such as *I'm sure, I'm positive, definitely*.

Example:
B: We have to increase production.
A: Well, we can definitely increase production if we hire more employees and buy better equipment.
B: Are you sure?
A: I'm positive.

Increase Production	Lower Costs
Hire more workers Buy new machinery Improve the production line	Change suppliers Use cheaper materials Have less overtime work
Increase Quality	**Increase Delivery Speed**

Work with a partner. Student B: Look at this page only. Student A: Look at page 105. Talk about the problems below. Choose a solution from the chart. Complete the chart with your partner's ideas. Use expressions such as *I'm sure, I'm positive, definitely.*

Example:

A: We have to increase delivery speed.

B: Well, we can definitely increase delivery speed if we hire more drivers and customer service people.

A: Are you sure?

B: I'm positive.

Increase Production	Lower Costs
Increase Quality Hire more people for quality control Improve production methods	**Increase Delivery Speed** Hire more drivers Hire more customer service people

D. Write two sentences for each problem. Use your ideas from Activity C.

Increase production

1. _____

2. _____

Lower costs

1. _____

2. _____

Increase quality

1. _____

2. _____

Increase delivery speed

1. _____

2. _____

Putting It to Work

1 Pair Work

Step 1. With a partner, listen to the meeting and complete the chart below.

Proposals	Problems
1. Increase overtime	1. Costs go up.

Step 2. With your partner, discuss the information in the chart and take a position for or against one of the ideas above.

Step 3. Talk to another pair of students and compare your ideas.

2 Pair Work

Step 1. With a partner, role-play a meeting between a supervisor and an employee. What has the employee done, and what has he or she not done? Use the notes below.

Report to Supervisor: Jobs for February	
Items	**Comments**
Repair drill press 14	Parts not available in Feb.
Replace wiring in area 3 ✔	Wiring—more than estimate
Replace parts in punch press 7 ✔	Punch press is now in perfect working order
Order new forklifts	Model has changed; new model is more expensive; order or not?

Step 2. Continue to role-play this situation: The supervisor suggests changes; the employee listens to the supervisor and agrees or disagrees.

Step 3. Continue with the situation. Can you agree on the employee's schedule and workload for the next month? Be flexible and try to agree, but don't give up on the important points.

3 Group/Class Work

Step 1. Form a group. Choose a team leader, a team recorder, and a team reporter. Consider the information below:

Fairview Hospital Supplies wants to accomplish the following:
- Increase production
- Lower costs
- Increase delivery speed
- Increase quality
- Increase sales

Step 2. Role-play a team meeting to make suggestions about these goals. Is it possible to achieve them all? Why or why not?

Step 3. Which goals are the most important? Which goals are possible? If one goal makes another goal impossible, you have to choose. Make a group list of priorities.

Step 4. Suggest ways to achieve the top priority goals. List your goals and suggestions on ways to achieve goals. If you need more space, use a separate sheet of paper.

Top Priority Company Goals

1. _____   3. _____

2. _____   4. _____

Ways to Achieve Goals

1. _____

2. _____

3. _____

Step 5. Your team reporter will tell your ideas to the class. With your class, evaluate the ideas of all of the teams.

4 Culture Work

Look at the pictures below. Meetings in companies are more formal than other kinds of contact on the job. Tell the class about your experiences.

Unit 10
SAFETY PROCEDURES

Openers

Look at the pictures. Point to the following things and signs:

No Smoking   Safety Meeting   a cigarette   a lighter

Fairview Hospital Supplies is having a safety meeting. Why do you think the company is doing this? Have you ever been to a safety meeting? What is usually discussed at a safety meeting?

1 Listen and Think

Listen and answer the questions with a partner.

1. What is Bud's job?

2. What is Bud's main responsibility?

3. Why does Bud ask Jorge for help?

4. What does Jorge tell Bud to do first?

5. Why is that so important?

2 Talk to a Partner

Step 1. Practice the conversation with a partner.

A: Hey! Watch out! Stop handling those
chemicals! Put them down!
B: Why?
A: You need to put on your goggles.
Those chemicals are very strong.
B: But I've been using them carefully.
A: I know. But if you accidentally
get some in your eyes, you'll burn them. In fact,
you could even go blind.
B: Oh! Thanks for the warning. I'll go
and get some goggles right now.

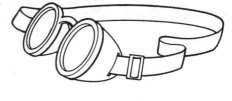

goggles

**Step 2. With the same partner, choose another type of protective clothing from the box.
Think about what each piece protects the employee from (chemicals, spills, fumes,
falling objects). Have a conversation like the one above.**

welding helmet   hard hat   gloves

3 Read and Think

Step 1. Read the text below.

Jorge went to a team safety meeting and learned about accident prevention in the workplace,
accidents that can be prevented by reading and following instructions and proper procedures. At
the meeting, safety signs that are posted around the company were explained to the employees.

  Some safety signs indicate something you must do or must not do in order to prevent an
accident. Other safety signs do not require any action, but they make you aware of a dangerous
situation that is present.

Step 2. With a partner, look at the safety signs below. Which ones require an action? Which ones provide information but do not require an action? Group the signs into two categories.

RADIATION

CAUTION

THIS DOOR MUST BE KEPT CLOSED

DANGER

HARD HAT AREA

CAUTION

RESPIRATOR REQUIRED IN THIS AREA

CAUTION

THIS DOOR MUST BE KEPT CLOSED

DANGER

HIGH VOLTAGE

DANGER

FLAMMABLE

CAUTION

THIS EQUIPMENT STARTS AND STOPS AUTOMATICALLY

NOTICE

EMERGENCY EXIT

Vocabulary

caution be careful

danger a warning of a risk that is present

proper procedures the way things should be done

posted hung up somewhere (on a wall, bulletin board, etc.) so people can read it

operate turn on and run something; for example, a machine

Step 3. Read the text below.

There are many safety signs posted in the workplace to remind employees to work safely throughout the day. Some reminders are general instructions for things employees should do. Some are directional signs, and these show where things are located. Directional signs often show an arrow pointing the way to something.

Step 4. Read the safety signs below. For each one, decide if it is a general reminder or a directional sign.

Walk—Don't Run

This Way Out

Fire Exit

Report All Unsafe Conditions to
Your Supervisor

To the Fire Escape

Report All Injuries No Matter How Slight

Help Keep This Plant Safe and Clean

Vocabulary

remind give information again that someone
already knows
plant factory
fire escape a stairway leading from upper floor
windows to the ground outside a building

slight small; little
report inform someone either orally or
in writing

Step 5. With a partner, read the safety information on the left below and match it to the correct place at work on the right.

Do Not Operate

Contents Pressurized

Harmful if Swallowed

This Space Must be Kept Clear at All Times

Make Your Workplace Safe Before Starting the Job

Keep Off—Electric Current

Label on container

Sign on wall

Sign on machine

Practice

Complete the sentences with the correct words.

exit   posted   operate   proper procedures   report

1. When I fell at work last week, I had to _____ *report* _____ it to my supervisor.

2. There are many safety signs _____ near the machinery.

3. If you don't follow the _____ when you work on machinery, you might get hurt.

4. You have to wear goggles when you _____ that equipment in order to protect your eyes.

5. When the fire alarm went off, we all stopped working and walked to the nearest

   _____.

4 Put It in Writing

Step 1. **Think of some safety procedures you follow either at work or at home. Imagine you have to explain the procedures to someone else. Write three sentences explaining what he/she must do.**

Example: *You must wear safety goggles.*

1. _____

2. _____

3. _____

Step 2. **Now add a reason to each sentence above.**

Example: *You must wear safety goggles to protect your eyes from chemicals.*

1. _____

2. _____

3. _____

5 Listen and Think

Step 1. Listen to the conversation.

A: What are you doing?
B: I'm moving this shipment to the back of the warehouse.
A: Yeah, but you're lifting wrong. If you keep lifting those heavy boxes like that, you'll hurt your back.
B: Listen. I've been doing it this way all my life and my back is fine.

Step 2. Practice the conversation with a partner.

Step 3. Continue the conversation.

Student A: Convince your partner to follow safety procedures.
Student B: You're very stubborn. Will you listen to your partner? Change roles.

What should you do if you see a co-worker do something dangerous? Should you say anything to him/her? Put yourself in the role of a supervisor. How would the conversation be different?

Step 4.   Discuss your opinions with another pair of classmates. Do you all agree?

6 Read and Write

Read the safety instructions. Rewrite each set of instructions as a series of steps.

A. Before turning on the machine, be sure the safety switch is on. You must wear safety goggles while operating this machine.

1. _____

2. _____

3. _____

B. Be sure the container is clean before pouring the chemicals in. Do not breathe in the fumes when mixing these chemicals. Wear a face mask. Never work with these chemicals without wearing rubber gloves.

1. _____

2. _____

3. _____

4. _____

Form and Function

1 Stop handling those chemicals!

Stop	**handling**	those chemicals!

I	**enjoy** **like** **hate**	**working.**	**Don't stop** **Start**	**working!**

Examples

Jorge **hates working** the night shift. He can't sleep during the day.
Susan **likes working** the night shift. She sleeps in the afternoon.
Most employees **don't like** working the night shift even though it pays a little more.

Practice 1

A. Listen. Circle the correct answer.

1. likes working   ⟨like working⟩   **4.** likes waiting   hates waiting

2. likes being   doesn't like being   **5.** don't like   doesn't like

3. likes having   doesn't like having   **6.** likes getting   like getting

B. Fill in the blanks with the correct forms of the verbs in parentheses. Use any other words in parentheses correctly in combination with the verbs.

1. Enrique (like) (work) _____*likes working*_____ in the maintenance department.

2. Rene (not) (like) (ask) _____ for help.

3. Everyone (like) (take) _____ breaks together.

4. Betty (hate) (park) _____ in the north parking lot because it's so dark.

C. Imagine your partner is doing one of the dangerous actions below. Warn him/her. Tell him/her to stop doing it.

- He/she is handling wires, and his/her hands are wet.

- He/she is welding, but he/she isn't wearing goggles.

2 I've been doing it this way all my life.

	I, you, we, they	**have**	**been doing** it this way.
	he, she, it	**has**	
	I, you, we, they	**haven't**	**been doing** it this way.
	he, she, it	**hasn't**	
Have	I, you, we, they		**been doing** it this way?
Has	he, she, (it)		
What have	I, you, we, they		**been doing**?
has	he, she, it		

Examples

Rhonda works in the laundry. She started five years ago. She **has been working** in the laundry for five years. She isn't in the union so she **hasn't been paying** dues.

Practice 2

A. Listen. Circle True or False. 🖭

1. Jim is a new employee.	T	(F)
2. We started waiting an hour ago.	T	F
3. I know what he said.	T	F
4. Colleen quit her job.	T	F
5. It rained this morning.	T	F

B. Combine the information given into one sentence.

Example: Tina is filling out an application. She started an hour ago.
Tina has been filling out an application for an hour.

1. Joe is working in the personnel office. He started a week ago.

_____

2. We are listening to the president on the radio. He started speaking forty minutes ago.

_____

3. Karl and Susan are working at the Edison Company. They were hired there thirty years ago.

_____

C. Think of three activities that you began sometime in the past that you are still doing. Write three sentences about the activities and how long you have been doing them. Then tell a partner about them.

Example: I have been painting my house for three weeks.

3 If you keep lifting those boxes like that, you'll hurt your back.

If	I, you, we, they he, she, it	**lift . . . ,** **lifts . . . ,**	I, you, we, they he, she, it	**will hurt** . . .
If	I, you, we, they he, she, it	**don't lift . . . ,** **doesn't get . . . ,**	I, you, we, they he, she, it	**won't hurt** . . . **won't earn** . . .

Examples

If you **leave** now, you**'ll arrive** on time. If we **don't leave** now, we**'ll be** late.
We**'ll miss** the beginning of the meeting **if** we**'re** late.
If John **works** hard, he**'ll get** a promotion. If John **doesn't work** hard, he **won't get** a promotion. He **won't get** a raise **if** he **doesn't work** hard either.

Practice 3

A. Listen. Circle the correct answer.

1. we will go to the beach
~~we won't go to the beach~~ (circled)

2. he'll be late
he won't be late

3. we'll miss our deadline
we won't miss our deadline

4. they'll come with us
they won't come with us

B. Work with a partner. Student A: Look at this page. Student B: Look at page 118. The chart below shows what two companies are offering Anna to work for them. Which offer should she accept? She needs to decide. Ask questions to complete the chart.

Example:

B: What will Anna's job be if she takes the job at Fairview?
A: She'll be a shift supervisor.

		Fairview	Fisher's
Job Title		shift supervisor	
Salary			$25,000
Schedule		3 PM–11 PM, Mon–Fri	
Vacation		1 week/year	
Sick leave			5 days/year
How many people she supervises		45	

Work with a partner. Student A: Look at page 117. Student B: Look at this page.
The chart below shows what two companies are offering Anna to work for them. Which offer should she accept? She needs to decide. Ask questions to complete the chart.

Example:

A: What will Anna's job be if she takes the job at Fisher's?

B: She'll be a department supervisor.

	Fairview	Fisher's
Job Title		department supervisor
Salary	$24,000	
Schedule		Mon–Fri, 8AM–5PM
Vacation		2 weeks/year
Sick leave	7 days/year	
How many people she supervises		15

C. Now write sentences about Anna's job offers.

1. _If Anna takes the job at Fisher's, she'll be a department supervisor._

2. _____

3. _____

4. _____

5. _____

6. _____

D. Role-play.

Student A: Pretend you are Anna. Think about the two job offers from the charts above. Ask your partner for his/her advice.

Student B: You are Anna's friend and you know she is a very hard worker. You want her to have the best job possible. Give her your opinion about the two job offers.

Putting It to Work

1 Pair Work

Step 1. Listen. With a partner fill in the missing information in the safety warnings you hear.

1. That's the fire _____*alarm*_____! Call the office and see if it's really a _____.

2. Hey, the _____ light just came on. Turn that machine _____.

3. Please proceed to the nearest _____ and leave the building.

4. A: Why is that _____ _____ flashing? B: I don't know.

   Let's look in the _____ manual.

5. _____ _____. There's some water on the floor over

Step 2. Discuss with your partner: Which of the warnings you heard indicate an emergency?

Step 3. Have you ever been in an emergency situation at work or someplace else? What happened? What did you do? Tell your partner about it.

2 Pair Work

Step 1. Role-play. Think of an emergency situation that might occur at work.

Student A: Imagine you are training a new employee and you must teach him/her what to do if this type of emergency ever happens.

Student B: You are a new employee. You have never been in an emergency situation before, so you have lots of questions to ask your trainer about what to do.

Example: A: Let me show you what to do in case the fire alarm goes off.
B: OK. Has there ever been a fire here?
A: No, but you need to know what to do, just in case. First, call the office to report the alarm.
B: Why do I have to do that?
A: They might not know the alarm is ringing.

Step 2. Use the information your trainer gave you and, together, write a list of steps to follow in case of emergency.

Step 3. Now it's your turn to train another pair of students. Use the list of steps you wrote and teach them what to do in case of emergency.

3 Group/Class Work

Step 1. Work in a group. Choose a team leader, a team recorder, and a team reporter. Imagine you are the safety committee for your company. Work together to design a plan for keeping your workplace safe. Provide the following information:

1. the type of company

2. the size of the company

3. the job titles of the safety committee members

4. the most common safety hazards at your company

Step 2. Design a plan for providing safety information to the company employees. Draw up any documents, charts, graphs, posters, etc. necessary to present the information to the employees.

Step 3. Your team reporter will present your safety information to the rest of the class. He or she will introduce the members of the committee and give background information on the company to the class.

Step 4. Give the class time to ask questions.

4 Culture Work

When should employers provide employees with safety information? Whose responsibility is safety in the workplace? Consider the following situations:

1. Ralph was walking down the hall at work when he noticed one of the light fixtures was loose.

2. Jan was operating a machine at work, and a warning light came on for a few seconds and then went off. This happened two or three times before lunch.

3. On his way in to work from the parking lot, Raymond saw two of the supervisors of the company. They were smoking near some pressurized tanks.

SAFETY FIRST

REPORT ALL UNSAFE CONDITIONS TO YOUR SUPERVISOR

What would you do in these situations? Discuss this question with the class.

Picture Dictionary

Jobs

a cashier

a chemist

doctors (physicians)

a machinist

a mechanic

a police officer

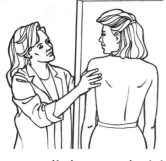

a radiology technician

a structural engineer

a warehouse worker

Tools and Protective Gear

goggles

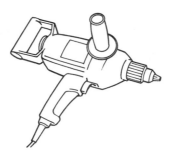

a power drill

a welding helmet

a welding torch

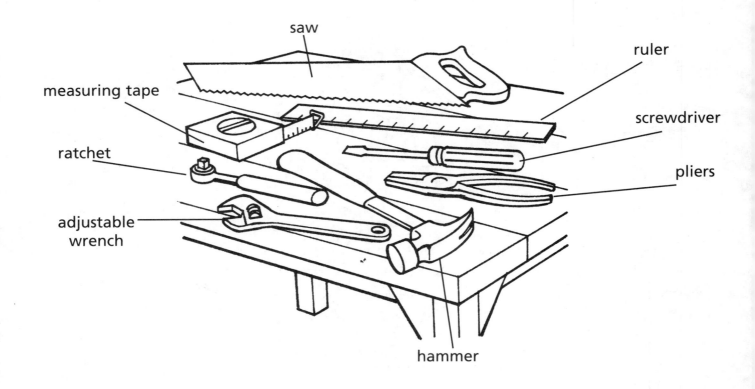

saw

ruler

measuring tape

screwdriver

ratchet

pliers

adjustable
wrench

hammer

Appendix

Abbreviations in Ads

Abbreviations appear in ads with periods and without periods. Here are some of the most common ones.

appt	appointment	f/t	full-time	p/t	part-time
bnfts	benefits	hrs	hours	ref	reference(s)
clk	clerk	mgr	manager	req	required
dr lic	driver's license	mo	month	sal	salary
EOE	Equal Opportunity	nec	necessary	temp	temporary
	Employer	oppty	opportunity	w/	with
eve	evening(s)	perm	permanent	wk	week (or work)
excel	excellent	pos	position	wpm	words per minute
exp	experience	pref	preferred	yrs	years